Copycat R

Quick & Easy Everyday Meals to Prepare in the Comfort of Your Home

Ursa Bourn

Table of Contents

Chapter 1- Introduction

Social eating is becoming a trend in our society today. We don't want to meet our friends just for their company, but our priority is to hang out somewhere where food is focused. We like to eat at lavish restaurants as well as fast food joints, purchase take-outs, snack at the cinema, eat at sports bars during football games, and nibble on popcorn at the movies. Today, diet and eating are ordinary socializing functions, not merely meals in support of wellbeing. However, it is generally believed that people who prepare food at home are inclined to eat less Calories: eat less carbs, consume less fats, and tend to be less obese. In the past few months, with Coronavirus leaving us more distant from each other, cooking at home is making a major resurgence. By having home-cooked meals as your diet, you will appreciate the health benefits of home cooking all the time, as well as enjoy being healthy with your friends and family.

1.1 Benefits of meals prepared at home

For improved wellness, introducing more home-prepared meals into everyday life is beneficial than consuming processed foods and restaurant meals. A few of the often underrated advantages of cooking are mentioned below.

1. You consume smaller Calories: without noticing the difference.

Restaurant meals can be high in fats and carbs, whereas processed food can be full of salt and chemicals. Cooked-at-home meals tend to be healthier and have less Calories: That's because once you start preparing meals for yourself, you choose the ingredients you select, and their quality as well as their quality, says diet advisor of the Wellbeing Project in New York.

When you cook, you become part of the food production chain from beginning to end: the food market to the mouth. You know all about the food you put into your body.

Therefore, you are less inclined to consume restaurant-sized meals that are often enough for two and less likely to indulge yourself in a cake or a drink. At home, we unconsciously approach the food differently, causing us somewhat unable to overeat and also likely to eat more healthily than we would if we were dining out,

A consistent diet of balanced, home-cooked food may also influence how you eat throughout the day. After all, if you get accustomed to consuming healthy, nutritionally balanced food at home most of the time, you may realize that you will be searching for it everywhere. Your kids will be more inclined to snack on carrots or fruit at a game or a party, even if they are offered junk food because they tend to snack on those items at home.

2. You become conscious of what you bring into your body.

Many people rush around or multitask while having a meal, which indicates they usually don't care about what they're eating. However, as you sit down at the table and enjoy your prepared meals, odds are you can eat in a more aware manner, recognizing the various tastes and ingredients in your meal. "When you're cooking, you know what's going in your food from start to finish. It keeps you much more in sync with the food you are putting into your body.

Experience and enjoy the process of eating to make you feel focused. Thoughtfully Eating just one bite can make us get back to the moment, letting go of the whirlpool of thoughts that are often caught up in our minds, and realizing that a clearer, simpler, more responsive way of being is just a breath or a bite away

3. You will interact with your loved ones.

Investing time with friends and family is vital to everybody's wellbeing. It reduces depression, which has been associated with loneliness, heart failure and other diseases. With a little initiative, cooking will help you feel more social. Invite your children to help you prepare food, giving them easy tasks if they are young or cook at a get-together with friends. And if you like to meet new friends, who want to prepare their own meals to take up a cooking class where you might make a few friends and learn a few skills.

And, until a meal is ready, do not underestimate the social advantages you reap. E.g., at different events, Adele loves catering to her family and friends' home-cooked meals. "Generally, food is approached with big smiles and a willingness to return, she says. Pérez of Ohio, meanwhile, stresses the importance of exchanging nutritious home-cooked meals with needy neighbors. "Whenever I help someone, I know I am doing something positive and helping myself." she says "I feel better about giving than about getting."

Not able to cook food for a big group? Holding a potluck for colleagues will carry much of the same advantages. Robinson suggests inviting friends over with easy yet nutritious meals. "It is important to make these activities as convenient as possible for guests to join."

4. You are stimulating your brain.

Adele admits that in her day job, she just does not have any room for creativity. She jokes, "I am not an imaginative accountant." Although when she cooks, playing with spices and modifying recipes as she feels necessary, she gets the opportunity to practice her

imagination. "It brings me some satisfaction and I feel like I am utilizing a different portion of my brain."

Seniors will notice higher cognitive skills when they learn how to cook. "Cooking is a healthy, engaging hobby to help seniors keep active and utilize their minds," he notes, adding that acquiring new techniques and activities — like making a new recipe — could ward off a cognitive loss. And what's more, baking or cooking will also help develop seniors' self-confidence. "If they do not depend on the family for food, it brings them a feeling of dignity that they value," says Dr. Moore. (He states that caregivers for seniors struggling with a cognitive disability should remain careful to take protective measures, for example, shutting off the gas stoves when they are not in use.)

Beyond satisfying your hunger, cooking is a great way to relax and connect with friends and family. It will even improve your emotional and physical wellbeing — advantages you'll reap well after the meal is finished.

1.2 Health benefits of home-cooked meals

Nutritionally balanced - Restaurants are known to be extremely high in Calories: carbohydrates, fats, sugars, and sodium both in fast foods and otherwise, and may also constitute low nutritional value. A really high level of fats and sugars can be present in even the healthy and low-calorie alternatives. On the other hand, eating at home enables you to. Chop out what you may find excessive in your diet. You have control over the food that you cook and the food that you consume.

Expand knowledge of food - The food that fills your stomach is much more than just good taste. What people eat can cure, cause illness, or even cause pain, and one of the most crucial aspects of the health benefits of home cooking is learning this. You can learn about foods that are r low high in certain minerals, vitamins, and other nutrients when you cook your own meals. And when s you understand how to incorporate nutritious foods to gratify your palate, that's when you boost your creativity!

Truly appreciate your food – The precise act of cooking your own food can contribute to a new respect for the food you enjoy. Since thoughtless munching and psychological eating can lead to obesity and type 2 diabetes, this is very relevant because you are not

fully aware of the foods you eat. Being more mindful of what you are consuming as you cook will help you least likely binge eat.

Ideal portions - Restaurants are known for their outrageous portions, which can contribute to America's massive overeating way of life and obesity problem. A study published by the International Publication of Obesity found that it had a little effect on food preference when they provided nutrition labels on regular menus. The opportunity to practice portion control and potentially reduce the temptation to overeat is facilitated when preparing food at home.

Build healthy habits - By cooking at home, you will build a healthier lifestyle. Through eating healthily, learning to cook, keeping to a meal schedule, the whole family can have an inspiration to live a balanced lifestyle.

Encourages family bonding - family meal time enhances family connections and strengthens family partnerships and relationships. Children benefit massively from the practice of cooking and consuming meals together. It is also a wonderful learning opportunity for parents to foster their kids with healthy eating habits. Many studies published by the University of Wisconsin found that eating meals with family at the dinner table is directly connected to fewer mental disorders, greater academic achievement in children and encouraged family sociability.

Food safety- Food poisoning (or food-borne illnesses) affect every 1 in 6 Americans annually, as per the CDC. Preparing food at home will provide you the sense of confidence you need to realize that you have used the freshest products, and you can be assured that you know that your food has indeed been stored and prepared at the right temperature.

Food allergy and sensitivity awareness- We have discussed that you regulate the nutritional consumption of your meals, preparing food for your family and yourself also provides control to prevent food allergens. Nuts and gluten are common food allergies, and all of these are prevalent and usually popular ingredients in many meals.

Hygiene- At home, you know what is in your food and how hygienic your food gives you a clean conscience. But you would want to ensure, of course, that your utensils, kitchen and tableware are sterile and that your ingredients are thoroughly prepared before eating.

Saves money- It is expensive to eat dinner in restaurants! Purchasing groceries is far more cost-effective than placing an order for take-out every other day. Yet there is a lot of controversy about whether a home cooked meal is cheaper than eating out, but when nutrition and the serving size are considered, eating-in saves you a lot more money! This strategy for saving money will keep improving your finances and reduce your levels of stress.

1.3 Ready to prepare your own meals?

The measures below will motivate you to become a modern and creative home cook.

Keep Stock

If you think you are too busy to cook, assess how busy you actually are and if that is really true. Taking a week to note down however long you have been surfing the website, watching Television, or playing games on your tablet. When you calculate all of the days, it would also be noticed you have more spare time. Schedule that downtime to whip up some nutritious recipes.

Form a Relationship with Your Kitchen

A cared-for and functional kitchen is a far more attractive place than the one that is grim and uninviting. By investing in certain essential cooking equipment and implementing an organizational structure that works for you, you can create a place where you can feel good.

Keep a hand on the basics.

Cooking becomes less of an ordeal if you do not have to regularly rush to the supermarket to buy a single item that you are missing. Store your most frequently used products in the pantry (such as pasta, flour, cooking oils, spices, and baking soda) so that you can cook with anything and anytime you want.

Planning ahead

Every weekend, spend a portion of the time preparing meals and making shopping lists for the whole week. Take your weekly routine into consideration: If you notice that Tuesday will be stressful, prepare for a meal that is fast and simple to make. You can customize preparing a meal on the busiest weeks with a little foresight.

Cook Extra

To regularly eat home-cooked food does not mean that you have to cook each night. Cut a break by preparing food large batches of each meal that you make to heat it up during the week (or freeze it and eat it down the road). Consider prepping items that can be recreated in various ways, such as roasted chicken breasts that can be used over a few days in pasta, in sandwiches, or with salads.

Keeping it simple

If you are totally new to meal preparation, don't assume like you have to be a professional chef every evening. Take baby steps and dedicate each week to cooking either one or two simple meals at home. Use basic ingredients (a classic example is pasta with red sauce), and grant yourself time in the kitchen to get comfortable.

Make food You Like to Eat.

Even if you are in charge of preparing a meal, do not feel intimidated to get fancy. If you like truffle oil-coated bacon duck breast, then do it. But the meal does not need to be reinvented. If a burger is more of your style, then create a homemade option for yourself. You will be quite likely to adhere to home cooking when you prepare meals you would like to eat.

Make It Social.

Cooking should not have to be a solitary thing. Invite everyone to the kitchen to reduce the amount of time and work required to cook the meal to make it more pleasant. Cooking with others is a perfect opportunity to connect and exchange knowledge in the kitchen and create new culinary discoveries.

Recognize Your Heritage.

Food is an important aspect of life. Reconnect to your roots through learning about your own traditional dishes. If you are unaware of where you originate from, this represents a remarkable chance to explore your ancestry.

Planting a garden

Growing food at home helps a person to be more in sync with the food they eat. And there is nothing more fulfilling (or nutritious) than consuming a salad made of produce harvested from the ground yourself. If you're going to plan it all, also learn about food storage techniques in winters and composting. Having your home cooking underway is just one advantage of investing in your property.

Try using a slow cooker.

Crockpots are an ideal investment for the beginner cook who may not have time or the culinary expertise to bring together a dinner. Combine the recipes in the morning to have a perfect dinner ready when you come home.

Get recipes or a cookbook.

Check out a range of cookbooks, recipe pages, or even take some lessons on the topic so you can create your own special cooking style.

Copycat recipes are a blessing to home cooks who like to reduce money spending or don't have the patience for a night out at a restaurant. There is still something so profoundly rewarding about developing a familiar taste in your kitchen, particularly if someone already has done the reverse engineering for your benefit. From your favorite cheesecake factory and Disney goodies to the beloved chain restaurant classics, we've compiled the largest, easiest, and most tasty copycat recipes in one location.

Whether you like to replicate the chili from Wendy, Jaipur veggies from Trader Joe, Starbucks' Spice Latte or something else, you would definitely find what you are craving for.

1.4 Conversion Chart

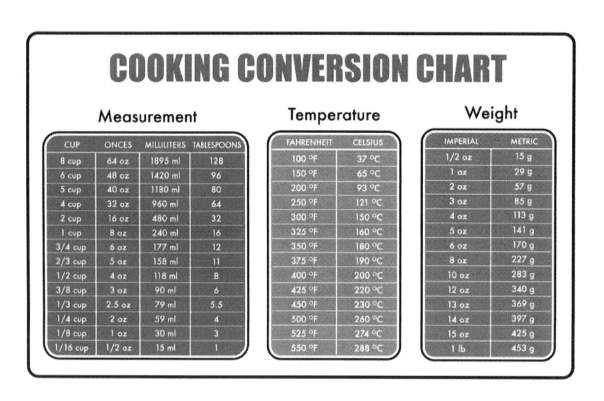

COOKING CONVERSION CHART

Measurement

CUP	ONCES	MILLILITERS	TABLESPOONS
8 cup	64 oz	1895 ml	128
6 cup	48 oz	1420 ml	96
5 cup	40 oz	1180 ml	80
4 cup	32 oz	960 ml	64
2 cup	16 oz	480 ml	32
1 cup	8 oz	240 ml	16
3/4 cup	6 oz	177 ml	12
2/3 cup	5 oz	158 ml	11
1/2 cup	4 oz	118 ml	8
3/8 cup	3 oz	90 ml	6
1/3 cup	2.5 oz	79 ml	5.5
1/4 cup	2 oz	59 ml	4
1/8 cup	1 oz	30 ml	3
1/16 cup	1/2 oz	15 ml	1

Temperature

FAHRENHEIT	CELSIUS
100 °F	37 °C
150 °F	65 °C
200 °F	93 °C
250 °F	121 °C
300 °F	150 °C
325 °F	160 °C
350 °F	180 °C
375 °F	190 °C
400 °F	200 °C
425 °F	220 °C
450 °F	230 °C
500 °F	260 °C
525 °F	274 °C
550 °F	288 °C

Weight

IMPERIAL	METRIC
1/2 oz	15 g
1 oz	29 g
2 oz	57 g
3 oz	85 g
4 oz	113 g
5 oz	141 g
6 oz	170 g
8 oz	227 g
10 oz	283 g
12 oz	340 g
13 oz	369 g
14 oz	397 g
15 oz	425 g
1 lb	453 g

Chapter 2- Breakfast Recipes

1. Five Ingredients Pancake- Cracker Barrel Copycat

This Cracker Barrel Breakfast recipe is much simpler than the typical pancake recipes out there. This recipe only includes five ingredients and 5 minutes, creating fresh pancakes in no time. (Additional directions below the formula for turning this recipe into a pancake mix also provided.)

Prep Time: 5 minutes | Cook Time: 10 minutes

Calories: 255 kcal | Servings: 6

Ingredients:

Pancakes

- Buttermilk, low fat (not anything more than 1%) 2 1/3 cups

- Eggs 2

- All-purpose flour (measure with a spoon, do not sift) 2 cups

- Granulated sugar 3tbsp

- Baking soda 2tsp

- Salt 1tsp

- Butter for cooking

Pancake Mix

- All-purpose flour (measure with a spoon, do not sift) 10 cups

- Granulated sugar1 cup

- Baking soda 2 Tbsp. plus 1 tsp.

- Salt 5tsp

Directions

To Make Pancakes

1. Heat a pancake griddle up to 350. Take off the paper from one side of the stick of butter and place it on a plate near the griddle for oiling.

2. Beat buttermilk and eggs together in a mixing bowl. Into it, add flour*, sugar, salt, and baking soda. Mix until just combined.

3. Oil the griddle with butter and pour half a cup of batter onto the buttered griddle. Use a big ice cream scooper for this purpose. Level out the batter when it hits the griddle and smooth it swiftly into a circle.

4. Flip the pancake when bubbles appear all over it, around 2 minutes. Cook the flipped side until the pancake has firmed up and golden.

5. Butter the griddle every time you pour on new batter.

6. Serve the pancakes piping hot; keeping them in an oven or stacking them up will make them soggy, or they may even become tough.

To Make a Pancake Mix:

By following this recipe, you'll be able to get pre-made pancake mix available anytime you need it. Before you realize it, you will find yourself regularly enjoying these delicious pancakes. You might mix up six to twelve pancakes at a time. I notice that six adults feed two citizens reasonably complete. When you prepare more than 12 pancakes at a time, the batter becomes more difficult to mix. Additionally, be sure to immediately prepare the batter as it won't cook well if you leave it to stay for an extended period. The remaining batter should be disposed of.

1. Mix together all the dry ingredients and store them in a sealed container with the cooking instructions.

2. To prepare 6 pancakes, beat together 1 egg with 1 cup plus 1 Tbsp. buttermilk. Slowly mix in 1 cup of pancake mix and prepare as directions above.

3. To prepare 12 pancakes, whisk together 2 eggs with 2 1/3 cups of buttermilk (low fat). Slowly mix in 2 cups of pancake mix and prepare as directions above.

Notes

Putting the flour into the measuring cup with a spoon and then level it off is the best way to measure. It ensures that you do not get too much flour into these soft pancakes.

This recipe will make 12 pancakes. Most adults will eat 2 to 3, and a child will most likely get filled with one.

2. Hash Browns- Waffle House Copycat

Perfect hash browns diners and restaurant-style!

Prep Time: 2 ½ hours | Cook Time: 15 minutes

Calories: 340 kcal | Servings: 4

Ingredients

- Potatoes, peeled and shredded 4 cups

- Salt 1 teaspoon

- Vegetable oil, for frying

- Ice 1 cup

- Water

Directions

1. In a large bowl, place the shredded potatoes. Pour in water, enough to cover the

potatoes add ice and salt. Mix in the salt by stirring.

2. Place the bowl in the refrigerator, covered, for 2 hours.

3. Pour the soaked potatoes into a strainer. Wash with cold water and strain completely. Pat them dry with a kitchen towel. Do not press too much.

4. On medium flame, heat a big frying pan. Pour just enough vegetable oil to coat the pan's bottom lightly.

5. When the frying pan is hot, place the drained potatoes into the frying pan and spread them around evenly (do not try to press them, or it will get soppy).

6. Without stirring, fry until crispy on the bottom; it will take about 12 to 15 minutes. Don't cover the pan while cooking. When golden, carefully turn them over and fry for 3 to 5 more minutes.

3. Homemade Sausage and Egg Muffin - McDonalds copycat

Here is the copycat edition of McDonald's Egg & sausage McMuffin. These sausage patties are produced from scratch, and they taste very close to the McDonald's sausage patty. These are the real thing! Perfect make-ahead breakfast- so simple and convenient.

Prep Time: 10 minutes | Cook Time: 15 minutes

Calories: 453 kcal | Servings: 4

Ingredients

For Sausage Patties

- Beef (mince) or ground pork (juicier) 1 lb. / 500g (Note 1)

- Dried ground sage 1/2 tsp

- Garlic powder (or onion powder) 1 tsp

- Dried thyme 1/2 tsp

- Black pepper 3/4 tsp

- Sugar 1/2 tsp

- Salt 3/4 tsp

For Muffins

- Oil 2 tbsp.

- Eggs 4

- English muffins, cut in half 4

- Cheese 4 slices, (Note 3)

Directions

Muffins

1. Heat oven up to 130C/275F

2. On a baking tray, Place muffins, cut side up and cover with cheese. (optional- place on sausage patties to melt the cheese)

Sausage Patties

1. In a bowl, combine all sausage Patty ingredients, using your hands to mix it really well!

2. Make them into 4 thick patties or 5 Mcsize patties. Try to make them a bit bigger than the muffins as they will decrease in size when cooking.

3. In a big nonstick frying pan, heat oil on high heat. Place the patties in the frying pan, do not overcrowd. Fry one side until browned or for 2 to 3 minutes. Turnover, then cook until the other side is also browned (or top with cheese, after flipping, covering with a lid to melt).

Egg

1. In the meantime, heat one more pan on medium-high flame with 1 tbsp. oil. Spray the egg rings with the oil and set them in the frying pan. (For more cook methods, see Note 4).

2. Break the eggs into the rings. Include about 2 tbsps. Water to the skillet and cover with a lid. Cook until eggs are cooked for 1 to 2 minutes or to your liking.

Assembling

From the oven, remove the warm muffins. Put the sausage on top, followed by the egg, and then the top of the muffin.

Serve immediately!

Notes:

- Meat-The meat being used for McDonald's sausage patties is different all over the world! In Canada and the US, pork is used, and in Australia, beef is used. Also, with the seasonings included, I guess people can't say! Pork patties are juicier, tastier and tenderer, so they reheat better.

- If using turkey, veal or chicken – the given seasoning goes well with all. For veal, increase the spices moderately.

- Cooking the eggs - to cook eggs in perfect shape, use the following:

- Tuna can: cut off the can's ends and wash properly. Use as a ring

- Always bake in well-oiled muffin tins

-use onion rings; it is best to cut the rings into 1/3 inch and use the larger outer rings.

- Otherwise, to make eggs oval, just break the eggs into a pan, and when it begins to heat, fold the edges in. Or you can either scramble them and create a big omelet and cut them to match into each.

- Cheese -use processed cheese to replicate McDonald's hamburgers.

- Make In advance: Keep refrigerated for up to four days, warm in the microwave on a low level for two minutes, or cover with aluminum foil and heat in the oven for five minutes.

- Freeze - create scrambled eggs or break into four. Freezing fried eggs are not a good idea as they will go rubbery.

4. Hash Brown Casserole- Cracker Barrel Copycat

This recipe is prepared for baking in a snap. All begins with homemade broth and finishes with a load of cheese. It's not going to get any better!

Prep Time: 10 minutes | Cook Time: 25 minutes

Calories: 453 kcal | Servings: 8

Ingredients

- Hash browns, shredded frozen 1 package (26 oz.)

- All-purpose flour, 4 Tbsp. Divided

- Poultry seasoning 1/4 tsp.

- Unsalted butter, cold 8 Tbsp. Divided

- Onion powder 1/4 tsp.

- Chicken broth, low-sodium 1 cup divided

- Garlic powder 1/4 tsp.

- Milk 1/2 cup

- Black pepper freshly ground 1/2 tsp.

- Chopped onions 1/2 cup

- Kosher salt 1/2 tsp.

- Colby cheese, shredded 1 package (8 oz.)

Directions

1. Heat oven up to 375 °F.

2. On medium heat, melt 2 tablespoons of butter in a medium sized pot. When the butter melts, add in 2 tablespoons of flour and all the seasonings. Mix to make a paste. Add in milk, stirring as you pour. Blend until completely mixed.

3. In a small mason jar, add chicken broth and 2 tablespoons of flour. Seal firmly and shake till you get a slurry - a smooth flour combination for thickening the sauce.

4. Gradually pour the slurry into the mixture in the pot, stirring constantly. Take to a boil and let cook for 2 minutes, whisking constantly.

5. Pour the sauce into a 9x13 casserole baking dish. Add the onions and remaining butter. Mix until the butter is melted. Add in frozen hash browns and cheese. Combine well.

6. Bake for 25 minutes or till the top is crisp and golden brown.

Serve hot!

Notes

If wanted, sprinkle on the casserole more cheese in the last 10 minutes of baking.

This recipe can be divided into 2 smaller casserole dishes.

5. Pan-Seared Pork Chops- Grandview Inn Bed & Breakfast Copycat

These easy and delicious pork chops are a quick recreation of breakfast served in Grandview Inn Bed & Breakfast. Served with a sunny side up egg, making it a wholesome meal.

Prep Time: 5 minutes | Cook Time: 6 minutes

Calories: 466 kcal | Servings: 4

Ingredients

- Pork chops, thin-sliced, bone-in 4
- Salt
- Paprika 2 tsp.
- Garlic powder 1 tsp.
- Onion powder 1 tsp.
- Dried thyme 1 tsp.
- Flour 1/2 cup
- Oil for frying (avocado oil, light olive oil) 2 tablespoons

Directions

1. Season both sides of the pork chops generously with salt.

2. Next, combine together the garlic powder, thyme, paprika, onion powder. Take the salted pork chops and rub this seasoning blend on both sides.

3. Dip the pork chops into the dry flour, and give them a decent shake to get clear of the excess flour.

4. On a medium-high flame, heat a large frying pan, then add about 2 tablespoons oil to layer the pan's bottom.

5. When the oil gets shimmering and hot, place the pork chops in one layer (cook in two batches), and fry for about 3 minutes on both sides, till golden brown. The temperature should be at least 145 degrees F when verified with an instant meat thermometer. Serve immediately!

6. Omelet - Ihop Colorado Omelet Copycat

Learn the easy way of making Colorado Omelet from IHOP with this cool copycat recipe. Relish the best omelet with ham, bacon, sausage, beef, veggies, and cheese.

Prep Time: 15 minutes | Cook Time: 6 minutes

Calories: 368 kcal | Servings: 2

Ingredients

- Butter 1 tablespoon

- Each diced and measured 1/4 cup

- Bell pepper

- Onions

- Tomatoes

- Bacon, fried

- Ham

- Breakfast sausage cooked and diced 1/3 cup

- Cheddar cheese shredded 3/4 cup

- Roast beef, shredded or deli roast beef, diced 1/3 cup

- Salt 1/4 teaspoon

- Eggs, beaten 4

- Water 1/8 cup

Directions

- On a medium-low flame, heat a saucepan and melt butter. Add in chopped bell peppers and onions. Keep stirring till just soft but not colored.

- Add in diced ham and keep stirring till the ham is heated through and limp. Remove from heat immediately and put aside.

- Take a mixing bowl to add in eggs, salt and water. Whisk them together well. Put the bowl aside.

- On medium-low flame, heat a 12-inch skillet, spray with a nonstick cooking spray.

- Pour the egg mix in the pan and scatter bell pepper, onions, tomato, ham if you desire, bacon, sausage, half of the roasted beef, and half a cup of cheese shredded.

- Cover with a lid on till the omelet begins to set. At that instant, take off the lid and start folding the omelet from the sides towards the middle (this seems difficult! Simply fold it in half).

- Sprinkling the roast beef and rest of the cheese heat until cheese melts. Garnish with sour cream and a few diced green onions.

Chapter 3- Salad Recipes

1. Oriental Chicken Salad- Applebee's Copycat

This appetizing Oriental Chicken Salad Copycat from Applebees is prepared with cabbage, breaded chicken, romaine, cucumber, crunchy chowmein, sliced almonds, and tossed in a tangy Asian dressing!

Prep Time: 10 minutes | Cook Time: 6 minutes

Calories: 1432 kcal | Servings: 2

Ingredients

- For Dressing
- Honey 3 tbsp.
- Rice wine vinegar 1 1/2 tbsp.
- Mayonnaise 1/4 cup
- Dijon mustard 1 tsp.
- Sesame oil 1/8 tsp.

For Fried Chicken

- Chicken breast 2

- Egg 1

- Milk 1 cup

- Flour 1 cup

- Panko 1 cup

- Salt 1 tsp.

- Pepper 1/4 tsp.

- Vegetable oil for frying 3 cups

- Ingredients for salad

- Romaine lettuce chopped 3 cups

- Carrot shredded 1

- Red cabbage chopped 1/2 cup

- Sliced almonds 3 tbsp.

- Napa cabbage chopped 1/2 cup

Directions

1. Prepare Dressing: Mix together all the dressing ingredients and chill till ready to serve.

2. Prepare Chicken: Heat oil in a large frypan on medium-high flame.

3. In the meantime, slice the chicken breast into long thin strips. Put aside.

4. Beat together milk and egg in a small bowl. In another bowl, mix the panko, flour, pepper and salt. Bathe the strips first in the egg mix, and then coat with flour completely.

5. Cautiously add the long chicken strips into the hot oil and fry until golden brown or cooked through for 3-4 minutes. Cool on a paper towel. When cool, cut into small pieces.

Prepare the salad:

1. Combine the red cabbage, romaine, carrots, napa cabbage, and cucumber.

2. Include the chopped chicken pieces and garnish with chowmein and almonds.

3. Pour the appetizing oriental honey dressing on top and enjoy!

2. Salad and Dressing - Olive Garden Copycat

You may skip the meal and eat the salad only if you try this amazing Olive Garden Salad. Making your own copycat salad dressing recipe at home is so simple. A crunchy salad with a sweet, cheesy and tart dressing will leave you wanting for more!

Prep Time: 10 minutes | Cook Time: 10 minutes

Calories: 632 kcal | Servings: 4

Ingredients

For Salads

- Romaine lettuce washed and chopped 3 hearts

- Roma tomatoes, sliced 2

- Parmesan cheese fresh shredded 1/4 cup

- Red onion sliced 1/2

- Pepperoncini pickled 4

- Seasoned croutons 1/2 cup

- Large black olives pitted 10

For Olive Gardens Copycat Dressing

- Mayonnaise 1/2 cup

- White vinegar 3 tablespoons

- Water 1/4 cup

- Sugar 1/2 teaspoon

- Olive oil extra light (or any neutral oil) 2 tablespoons

- Kosher salt 1/4 teaspoon

- Romano cheese, grated 2 tablespoons fresh

- Garlic powder 1/4 teaspoon

- Lemon juice, fresh 1/2 tablespoon

- Italian seasoning 1 teaspoon

Directions

1. Prepare Dressing: Blend together all the dressing ingredients until smooth and chill till ready to serve.

2. Assemble salad: Take a large salad bowl to layer the salad ingredients starting with the lettuce. Transfer the salad dressing onto the salad and mix to combine.

Serve immediately!

---

3. Chipotle Copycat

Prep Time: 15 minutes | Cook Time: 15 minutes

Calories: 160 kcal | Servings: 4

Ingredients:

- White sweet corn, fresh 16 ounces

- Poblano pepper 1 large

- High heat oil 1 teaspoon

- Red onion 1 small (approx. 3/4 cup)

- Jalapeno pepper 1

- Fresh cilantro 1/2 cup

- Juice of limes 2+ lemon 1 (approx. 1/2 cup)

- Sea salt large pinch

Directions:

1. Set the oven to broil and line tinfoil on a cookie tray. Coat the poblano peppers with

2. the oil and assemble them on the cookie tray. The oven broils the peppers for 5 to 7 minutes on both sides, making sure that it doesn't burn. When both the sides are brown, take off from the oven and put aside in a large container. Cover the container and let the pepper sit for about 15 minutes.

3. In the meantime, prepare the salsa by chopping finely the fresh cilantro, jalapeno pepper (seeds and core removed), and red onion. Put in a large bowl and keep aside.

4. When the pepper is cool, peel away the outer layer of the skin using your hands. Do not forget to put on dish gloves; otherwise, your hands may burn. Then cut the top off and slice away the flesh from the core. Chop the pepper finely and add it to the container with the corn.

5. Pour the lemon-lime juices into the container along with a big pinch of sea salt and mix till well combined. Add in more salt if required.

6. Serve immediately or refrigerate for up to 4 days.

4. Coleslaw- KFC Copycat

Prep Time: 5 minutes | Cook Time: 15 minutes

Calories: 230 kcal | Servings: 4

Ingredients

- Mayonnaise 1/2 cup

- Buttermilk 1/4 cup

- Sugar 1/3 cup

- Milk 1/4 cup

- Apple cider vinegar 1 tablespoon

- Lemon juice 2 tablespoons

- Salt 1/4 teaspoon

- Pepper 1/8 teaspoon

- Minced dried onion 1/2 tablespoon (or fresh minced onion 1 tablespoon)

- Cabbage shredded (and carrots) 1 bag

- Or

- Shredded carrots 1/4 cup

- Cabbage 1/2 head

Directions

1. In a large bowl, whisk together mayonnaise, sugar, buttermilk, milk, minced onion, lemon juice, vinegar, pepper, and salt. Combine until smooth.

2. Add the carrots and cabbage and combine well.

3. Cover and chill for 2-3 hours or until serving.

Chapter 4- Appetizers & Sauce Recipes

1. Chick-Fil-a sauce copycat

This Copycat Sauce is ideal for dipping chicken, fries, or whatsoever your heart craves. So easy to prepare at home.

Prep Time: 5 minutes | Cook Time: 0 minutes

Calories: 293 kcal | Servings: 2

Ingredients

- Mayonnaise ¼ cup

- Dijon mustard 2 tsp

- BBQ sauce 2 tbsp.

- Honey 2 tbsp.

- Yellow mustard 1 tbsp.

- Lemon juice squeezed fresh 2 tsp

Directions

1. Blend mayonnaise, mustards, honey, and BBQ sauce and lemon juice all together in a

bowl.

2. Chill in a covered container.

---

2. Mayonnaise - Hellman's Copycat

If you want to produce all your sauces from scratch or only need a tablespoon of mayonnaise, this Hellman's copycat is on the mark. Pro-tip: add in a little sriracha for spicy mayonnaise.

Prep Time: 10 minutes | Cook Time: 0 minutes

Calories: 104 kcal | Servings: 1.5 cups

Ingredients

- Egg (at room temp) 1

- Dry mustard 1 teaspoon

- Salt 1 teaspoon

- Oil (canola, vegetable, or corn) 1 1/4 cup

- Cayenne pepper 1 dash

- Vinegar or lemon juice 3 tablespoons

- Directions

- In a blender, add egg, 1/4 cup oil, salt, mustard, and cayenne pepper and blend on low.

As the machine is running, GRADUALLY pour 1/2 cup oil more into it. Stop the machine and clean down the sides of the blender with a rubber spatula. Include the vinegar or lemon juice and the leftover 1/2 cup oil. Keep blending till well combined.

Chill covered tightly.

3. Arby's Sauce and Sandwich– Arby's Copycat

With this Arby's sauce copycat recipe, you can create your own style of the fast-food fave!

Prep Time: 5 minutes | Cook Time: 20 minutes

Calories: 54 kcal | Servings: 12

Ingredients

- Organic Ketchup 1/2 Cup
- Apple Cider Vinegar 1 Tablespoon
- Water 4-6 Tablespoons
- Sea Salt 1/4 teaspoon
- Hot Sauce (Crystal or Tabasco) 4-5 Drops
- Onion Powder 1/4 teaspoon
- Brown Sugar 2 Tablespoons
- Garlic Powder 1/4 teaspoon

Directions

1. In a small saucepan, add all ingredients.

2. Cook on medium-low heat for 20 minutes. Stirring frequently, especially for the last 10 minutes, so it doesn't stick or burn.

3. Pour into an airtight jar and preserve it in the refrigerator.

4. To be consumed within 1 to 2 weeks.

5. Serve sauce with Roasted Beef Sandwiches.

6. Butter the Hawaiian Sandwich Buns lightly and grill, in a big frypan, till lightly golden.

7. In a pan, heat shredded deli roast beef for a minute

8. Fill the roast beef in the grilled buns and drizzle Arby's Sauce generously and cover with bun top.

9. Serve with home fried Arby's Curly Fries.

---

4. Sauce and Burger - Shake Shack Copycat

Prep Time: 10 minutes | Cook Time: 10 minutes

Calories: 540 kcal | Servings: 4

Ingredients

For sauce

- Mayo 1/2 cup

- Ketchup 1 tbsp.

- Cayenne pepper 1/4 tsp

- Yellow mustard 1 teaspoon

- Dill pickle brine 1 tbsp.

For burger

- Beef 1 lb. ground

- Lettuce 8 leaves

- Tomato 8 slices

- Hamburger potato buns 4

- American cheese 4 slices

- Butter 1 tablespoon

- Salt & pepper

Directions

1. Prepare the sauce: blend all of the ingredients of the sauce together in a bowl.

2. Prepare burger: divide the ground beef equally into portions of 4 oz. (it will make four patties).

3. With your hands, shape them into burger patties. Make them thin—they tend to shrink

while cooking.

4. Season both sides of the patties with pepper and salt.

5. Over medium heat, heat up a cast-iron pan. Once hot, add butter and melt it.

6. Fry the patties in the pan, cooking for 5 minutes on both sides.

7. Turn them over and press down with a flat metal spoon. Add the cheese slice.

8. Meanwhile, cut up the vegetables. Layer a good amount of sauce on the buns. Add lettuce leaves and tomato slices. Serve

5. Blooming Onion Flower -Outback Steakhouse Copycat

If you haven't tried a large fried onion, you are obviously missing out. They are not only delicious to eat, but they are also quick and fun to make.

Prep Time: 54 minutes | Cook Time: 6 minutes

Calories: 340 kcal | Servings: 4

Ingredients

- Mayonnaise 2 tablespoons

- Ketchup 1 1/2 teaspoons

- Worcestershire sauce 1/2 teaspoon

- Sour cream 2 tablespoons

- Horseradish, 1 tablespoon

- Eggs, 2 large

- Paprika 1/4 teaspoon

- Cayenne pepper, to taste

- Ground Black pepper

- Kosher salt

- Sweet onion (1 pound) 1 large

- Flour, all-purpose 2 1/2 cups

- Thyme dried 1/2 teaspoon

- Cayenne pepper 1 teaspoon

- Oregano dried 1/2 teaspoon

- Paprika 2 tablespoons

- Ground cumin 1/2 teaspoon

- Corn or soy oil 1 gallon

- Whole milk 1 cup

Directions

1. In a big mixing bowl, combine sour cream, horseradish, mayonnaise, ketchup, Cayenne pepper, Worcestershire sauce, paprika, black pepper and Kosher salt. Cover and chill.

2. To prepare the onion, slice off 1/2 inch from the end of the onion, and peel.

3. Place the onion on the cutting board cut-side down, starting 1/2 inch away from the root, cut all the way down.

4. Make four equally spaced cuts in the same manner all around the onion.

5. Keep slicing in between each cut part to make 16 cuts spaced evenly.

6. Flip the onion and lightly separate the outer layers using your fingers.

7. In another bowl, combine the flour, paprika, cayenne, oregano, thyme, cumin and half a teaspoon of black pepper, stir well.

8. Beat the milk, eggs, and one cup of water in yet another deep small bowl.

9. Place the onion, cut-side up in a dry bowl and empty all seasoned flour on top.

10. Cover the bowl with a tight lid or a plate and shake it back and forth to distribute the flour evenly.

11. Ensure that the onion and its layers are fully coated.

12. Lift the onion by its core, flip it over and dust the excess flour off.

13. Keep this flour bowl for the next step.

14. Now, with the help of a slotted spoon, submerge the onion fully in the egg mixture.

15. Take it out, drip off the excess egg, and again dip in the flour bowl, coating it completely.

16. Put the onion in the refrigerator to chill; meanwhile, heat the oil.

17. On a medium-high flame, heat the oil in a large deep pot till a deep-fryer thermometer reads 400 degrees Fahrenheit.

18. Pat off the excess flour of the onion.

19. Lower the onion, cut-side down, cautiously into the oil, with the help of a wire skimmer.

20. Regulate the oil temperature so that the heat stays near 350 degrees Fahrenheit.

21. Deep fry onion for about 3 minutes on both sides until golden.

22. Drain on a plate lined with paper towels.

23. Sprinkle salt to taste serving with the prepared dip.

6. Guacamole – Chipotle copycat

Presenting bits of red onion jalapeno and garden-fresh herbs that fleck the creamy avocado. Citrus liquids and salt fulfill this modest and fresh guac.

Prep Time: 10 minutes | Cook Time: 10 minutes

Calories: 170 kcal | Servings: 4

Ingredients

- Ripe avocados 8

- Jalapeño, (deveined, deseeded, and minced) 1 medium

- Fresh lemon juice 1 tablespoon

- Fresh red onion, minced 1/4 cup

- Kosher salt 1 teaspoon

- Cilantro chopped 2 tablespoons

- Fresh lime juice 1 teaspoon

Directions

1. Add cilantro, jalapeño, and onion in a standard size bowl. Cut avocados in halves and keep one pit in the bowl. Spoon out avocados one by one and add to the bowl. Add lime and lemon juices and salt. Mash the avocado with the help of a fork to preferred consistency.

2. Put the avocado pit in the guacamole to prevent it from oxidizing (and it really works). Press a plastic wrap on top of the guacamole till ready to serve.

7. Honeyed Chicken Crispers – Chipotle Copycat

These honeybunch chicken crispers are a chipotle chili's copycat. Crunchy fried chicken bites coated in a sugary and hot sauce.

Prep Time: 15 minutes | Cook Time: 15 minutes

Calories: 785 kcal | Servings: 4

Ingredients

- Chicken tenderloins 12

- Canola oil 6-8 cups

For Batter

- Egg 1

- Garlic powder 1/4 teaspoon

- Milk 1/2 cup

- Pepper 1/4 teaspoon

- Chicken broth ½ cup

- Salt 1¼ teaspoons

- Flour ¾ cup

- For crumbing

- Flour 1½ cups

- Salt 1 teaspoon

- Black pepper ½ teaspoon

- Paprika 1 teaspoon

- Garlic powder ½ teaspoon

For honey chipotle sauce

- Honey 2/3 cup

- Chipotle's chili powder 1-2 teaspoons

- Water ¼ cup

- Apple cider vinegar 1 tablespoon

- Ketchup ¼ cup

- Hot sauce ½ teaspoon

- Salt ½ teaspoon

Directions

1. Combine ketchup, honey, water, chili powder, vinegar, hot sauce and salt, in a small pan. Take it to a simmer and for 2 minutes, cook, stirring regularly. Take off from the heat.

2. In another bowl, blend together milk, egg, chicken broth, pepper, garlic powder and salt to make a batter. Mix in flour.

3. In a deep dish, mix all the ingredients for crumbing.

4. In a Dutch oven, heat oil up to 350 degrees F. Coat chicken in egg batter and then place on to crumbing plate and coat completely.

5. Fry a few pieces simultaneously, cook until golden brown and thoroughly cooked, for

about 4 minutes.

6. Shift fried chicken tenderloins to a large bowl and drizzle honey-chipotle sauce all over. Serve.

8. Copy Cat Cracker Barrel Buttermilk Biscuits

This method uses prepared pancake or biscuit mix to produce these delicious treats. Baking is demanding work. Have this recipe remove the complexity for a little while.

Prep Time: 10 minutes | Cook Time: 10 minutes

Calories: 286 kcal | Servings: 6

Ingredients

- Readymade pancake or biscuit mix 2¼ cup

- Buttermilk 2/3 cup

- Granulated sugar 1½ tsp.

- Unsalted butter melted 1 tbsp.+ 2 tbsp. for brushing

- All-purpose flour ¼ cup + more for dusting

Directions

1. Heat oven up to 450 degrees F and oil a baking dish with oil.

2. In a medium mixing bowl, mix together the readymade pancake or biscuit mix, sugar and buttermilk. Stir until well mixed.

3. Mix again, adding in a tablespoon of soft butter. Mix well.

4. Dust all-purpose flour on a flat surface. On it, knead the dough for at least 10 minutes.

5. Spread the dough till it is at a thickness of 1/2 inch to 1 inch all around. Cut with top of a round glass or a round cutter, transfer the cut rounds to a baking tray.

6. Apply melted butter on the tops with a brush.

7. Place in the oven for 8 to 10 minutes. Bake till the tops are golden brown. Remove from the oven and apply the leftover melted butter on the tops with a brush.

Notes

If the dough appears sticky once everything is mixed, add a bit of all-purpose flour.

9. Breadsticks - Pizza Hut copycat

The recreation of Pizza Hut's iconic breadsticks, soft and buttery, with loads of seasoning!

Prep Time: 1 hour 50 minutes | Cook Time: 10 minutes

Calories: 186 kcal | Servings: 20 breadsticks

Ingredients:

For The Dough:

- Dry milk powder, non-fat ¼ cup

- Granulated sugar, 1 tablespoon

- Instant yeast, rapid-rise 2¼ teaspoons

- Salt ½ teaspoon

- Warm water 1⅓ cups

- Olive oil 2 tablespoons

- Bread flour 4 cups

For the dipping sauce:

- Tomato sauce 15 ounce can

- Granulated sugar 1 teaspoon

- Dried oregano 1 teaspoon

- Dried basil ½ teaspoon

- Dried marjoram ½ teaspoon

- Garlic powder ½ teaspoon

- Salt ¼ teaspoon

- Seasoning for the breadstick:

- Parmesan cheese, grated 2 tablespoons

- Onion powder 1 tablespoon

- Dried oregano 1 tablespoon

- Garlic powder 1¾ teaspoons

- Dried basil 1½ teaspoons

- salt ½ teaspoon

- Unsalted butter, melted, divided, 12 tablespoons

Directions:

1. Prepare the dough: Put the sugar, dry milk powder, salt and yeast in a bowl of the stand mixer fixed with a dough hook. Include the water and combine well. Leave it to sit for about 2 to 5 minutes. The mixture will start to bubble. Include the olive oil and mix again.

2. Start the machine on low speed; slowly add the flour till a dough starts to form. Knead on a medium-low speed till a soft but slightly sticky dough is formed, and it leaves the sides of the mixing bowl in about 5 minutes. Transfer the dough to a surface that is floured lightly and split in two.

3. Brush two 9x13-inch pans with 4 tablespoons of melted butter in each. Shape both pieces of dough into a rectangle of 9x13-inch and shift to each pan. Apply a tablespoon of melted butter on each dough. Cover tightly with plastic wrap and leave in a warm place until almost double in size, for about 90 minutes.

4. Prepare the Dipping Sauce: As the dough is resting, make the dipping sauce. Stir together the sugar, tomato sauce, oregano, marjoram, basil, salt and garlic powder in a small saucepan. Cook over medium heat till the sauce starts to boil, then decrease the heat to low and cook for about 30 minutes, stirring sometimes. Take off from the heat.

5. Make the Breadsticks: Heat the oven up to 475 degrees F.

6. When the dough rises, take off the plastic wrap and cut both the doughs into 10 equal breadsticks with a pizza cutter's help. Bake them until the edges start to crisp up and

are golden brown, about 10 to 15 minutes.

7. Prepare the Breadstick Seasoning: As the breadsticks are baking, start with the breadstick seasoning. Mix together the onion powder, Parmesan cheese, garlic powder, oregano, salt and basil in a small mixing bowl.

8. Once the breadsticks are done, take them out from the oven, brush both pans with the leftover melted butter, and generously sprinkle on the breadstick seasoning immediately. Let cool in the pan for 5 to 10 minutes. Slide the breadsticks with the help of a spatula onto a cutting board. Cut breadsticks with a knife or a pizza cutter and have warm or at room temperature. Serve with the prepared dipping sauce.

Note:

You can also knead and mix this breadstick dough by hand. It needs to be kneaded until an even, slightly sticky ball is formed.

10. Corn Dogs - Disneyland Copycat

With a fluffy, light breading seasoned with a touch of sweetness, fried to a crispy golden brown, you will be amazed how simple these can be made at home!

Prep Time: 10 minutes | Cook Time: 30 minutes

Calories: 340 kcal | Servings: 10

Ingredients

- Hot dogs 10
- Cornmeal 1 cup
- Granulated sugar 2 tablespoon
- All-purpose flour 1 cup
- Baking powder 2 teaspoon

- Buttermilk, 1 cup + more for consistency 1-3 tbsp.

- Salt 1/2 teaspoon

- Egg 1

- Honey 2 tablespoon

- Wooden sticks 10

- Vegetable oil, 2 quarts divided

Directions

1. Combine cornmeal, baking powder, flour, salt and sugar in a large mixing bowl,

2. Add egg, buttermilk, 2 tbsp. of vegetable oil, and honey to the bowl with the dry ingredients and beat until combined thoroughly. Put the bowl aside and leave the batter to rest for 10 minutes.

3. Meanwhile, in a deep, large, skillet heat the vegetable oil for deep frying, up to 350 degrees F

4. Insert wooden popsicle sticks into the hot dogs, leave some room at the bottom of the sticks to hold on to while also holding the hot dog securely in place. If necessary, pat dry the hot dogs with a paper towel.

5. Stir the corn dog batter. It must be thick enough to coat a spoon and be liquid enough to slowly trickle off. If the batter gets too thick, add a tablespoon of buttermilk and mix to even out the consistency, then perform another drip test. Add up to 3 tbsp. of buttermilk.

6. In a tall glass, pour the corn dog batter to at least 3/4 full. Hold the hot dog by the stick and immerse into the batter. Twist gently to coat the hot dog completely, gently pull it out, shaking off any extra batter.

7. Lightly drop it by the stick into the oil. Fry the corn dog for 3 to 5 minutes, turn the corn dog using tongs as needed. Transfer the corn dogs to a plate lined with a paper towel. Apply batter and cook all corn dogs in the same way.

Serve immediately with sauces of your choice.

11. Avocado Egg Rolls - Cheesecake Factory Copycat

It's so easy and cheaper to prepare at home and is a million times tastier too!

Prep Time: 15 minutes | Cook Time: 5 minutes

Calories: 288 kcal | Servings: 8

Ingredients:

- Vegetable oil 1 cup

- Avocados, halved, peeled and seeded 3

- Roma tomato, diced 1

- Diced red onion 1/4 cup

- Cilantro leaves fresh chopped 2 tablespoons

- Lime juice 1

- Kosher salt and

- Black pepper ground fresh, to taste

- Egg roll wrappers 8

For the dipping sauce

- Cilantro leaves, fresh loosely packed 3/4 cup

- Sour cream 1/3 cup

- Juice of 1 lime

- Mayonnaise 2 tablespoons

- Jalapeno, deveined and seeded, optional 1

- Garlic 1 clove

- Black pepper, fresh ground, to taste

- Kosher salt

Directions:

1. Prepare the cilantro dipping sauce by combining cilantro, jalapeno, sour cream, mayonnaise, lime juice and garlic in the bowl; add pepper and salt to taste. Put aside.

2. In a Dutch oven or large fry pan, heat vegetable oil on medium-high flame.

3. Softly mash avocados with a fork or a potato masher in a medium mixing bowl. Add red onion, tomato, lime juice, cilantro, pepper and salt, taste, and mix.

4. Take an egg roll wrapper, put the avocado mixture in the middle. Folding in the sides, take the lower side of the wrapper and fold firmly over the filling. Keep rolling up until the topmost of the wrapper is touched. With your finger, apply water to the edges of the wrapper, seal by pressing. Make all the rolls in the same way.

5. Cook in batches, deep fry the egg rolls until crispy and golden brown all over, for about 2 to 3 minutes. Shift to a plate lined with a paper towel.

6. Serve hot with the cilantro dipping sauce.

Chapter 5- Soup Recipes

1. Chicken Gnocchi Soup - Olive Garden Copycat

The orange color of the soup comes with the freshly grated carrot, but that's normal!

Prep Time: 15 minutes | Cook Time: 20 minutes

Calories: 230 kcal | Servings: 4

Ingredients

- Celery ribs 4

- Large carrot 1

- White onion 1/2

- Garlic cloves 6

- Olive oil 2 tablespoons

- Chicken breast 1 large

- Chicken broth 4 cups

- Salt 1 1/2 tablespoons

- Pepper 1 1/2 tablespoons

- Garlic powder 1 1/2 tablespoons

- Onion powder 1 tablespoon

- Thyme 1 tablespoon

- Gnocchi 2 cups

- Half and half 2 cups

- Cornstarch 2 tablespoons

- Parmesan cheese, shredded for garnish

Directions

1. Heat the oven up to 350 degrees F.

2. Sprinkle a half tablespoon of salt, garlic powder and black pepper on the chicken breast to season. Put the chicken in the preheated oven for about 10 minutes, or verify that the internal temperature reaches 145 degrees F on a meat thermometer.

3. Mince garlic, shred the carrots and chop the onion and celery.

4. On medium heat, add olive oil to a large pot. Add in the chopped vegetables and cook for around 4 minutes.

5. Then add in the cooked & chopped chicken breast and mix with the vegetables.

6. Pour in the chicken broth, also adding 1 tablespoon of salt, garlic, ground pepper, onion powder, and thyme. Stir all together, and then let the mixture come to a boil.

7. When the mixture begins to boil, include the gnocchi in it. Let it boil for around 3 minutes.

8. Then, decrease the heat and cover the pot. Let the mixture simmer for 10 minutes. Then take off the lid and stir, adding 2 cups of half and half.

9. Form a paste of 2 tablespoons cornstarch with 1 tablespoon water to ensure the cornstarch is totally dissolved. Then add this mixture to the soup that will thicken the broth.

10. Lastly, turn the stove off and serve the soup. You can also sprinkle some parmesan

cheese. Serve & enjoy with breadsticks!

2. Walkabout Soup - Outback Steakhouse Copycat

This copycat version of Walkabout Soup is delightful, heartening, and just as worthy as the original!

Prep Time: 5 minutes | Cook Time: 1 hour 30 minutes

Calories: 417 kcal | Servings: 6

Ingredients

- Chicken stock low sodium 10 cups

- Heavy cream 1 cup

- Bay leaves, fresh or dry 2

- All-purpose flour sifted 1 cup

- Yellow onions, sweet, quartered & sliced thinly 2 large

- White cooking wine ¼ cup

- White onion, large, quartered & sliced thinly 1

- Monterey jack cheese shredded ½ cup + extra for garnish

- Cheddar cheese, shredded, extra sharp, 1 cup + extra for garnish

- Black pepper freshly ground to taste

- Salt to taste

Directions

1. Add the cooking wine, chicken stock, onions and bay leave in a 4-quart stockpot. On high heat, bring it to boiling, and then decrease the heat to let it simmer. Simmer for one hour, uncovered.

2. Take out bay leaves, then gently mix in the dry flour till a small number of clomps of flour can be seen. Simmer the soup for at least 30 minutes.

3. Include the Monterey & cheddar cheeses, cream, and keep stirring till all the cheese is

   melted. Take off from the heat. Sprinkle pepper & salt to taste.

4. Garnish with additional cheese and serve as.

---

3. Vegetable Soup – Cracker Barrel Copy Cat

This healthy, hearty soup makes 5-6 quarts enough to fill the hungry tummies of a big family.

Prep Time: 15 minutes | Cook Time: 1 hour

Calories: 150 kcal | Servings: 10

Ingredients

- Water 5 cups

- Beef bouillon 4 cubes

- Vegetable juice (e.g., v8) 5 cups

- Celery, sliced2 stalks

- Russet potatoes peeled & cubed 2 large

- Green beans, normal cut with the juices, 1 can (16 oz.)

- Diced tomatoes 2 cans (14 oz.)

- Frozen onions 1 bag (10 oz.)

- Frozen bags of the following: 1 bag (about 12 oz. Each)

- Corn

- Lima beans

- Peas

- Salt 1 tsp.

- Ground pepper 1 tsp. (adjust according to your taste)

Directions

1. Add everything to a large stockpot, mix and take to a boil.

2. Decrease heat to medium – let it simmer. Cook covered for about 1 hour.

Notes

It can also be made in a slow cooker. It'll need to pretty much cook all day on high to have the potatoes soft enough to enjoy.

---

4. Sausage and Lentil Soup - Carrabba's Copycat

Sausage and Lentil soup is a tasty meal. It's like a favorite restaurant comfort meal but simpler to cook at home. Carrabba's Sausage & Lentil Soup becomes a favorite at everyone's home! So delicious!

Prep Time: 10 minutes | Cook Time: 1 hour

Calories: 219 kcal | Servings: 8

Ingredients

- Italian sausage 1 lb.

- Garlic minced 3 cloves

- Onion, diced 1 large

- Celery chopped 1 stalk

- Carrots chopped 2 large

- Zucchini chopped 1 small

- Chicken broth 5 cups

- Diced tomatoes, undrained 2 cans (14.5 ounces)

- Dry lentils 2 cups

- Salt 2 teaspoons

- Pepper 2 teaspoons

- Fresh oregano and basil for garnish

- Shredded parmesan for garnish

Directions

1. On a medium-high flame, brown sausage in a large pan, crumbling it as you cook. Once the sausage is nearly done, include garlic and keep cooking.

2. Take a Dutch oven or a large stockpot to mix all the ingredients and bring it to boil.

3. Decrease the heat to let simmer covered.

4. Simmer until lentils are done or for about 1 hour. If soup gets too thick, add a little water till it reaches desired consistency.

5. Sprinkle basil, oregano, and garnish with parmesan.

Chapter 6- Pasta Recipes

1. Mac & Cheese - Chick fil A copycat

Making these creamy and cheesy mac & cheese same as Chick-fil-A at home is a breeze!

Prep Time: 5 minutes | Cook Time: 30 minutes

Calories: 494 kcal | Servings: 12

Ingredients

- Macaroni 16 ounces

- Salt 1 tablespoon

- Parmesan cheese 2 tablespoons

- American cheese 1 1/4 pounds

- Romano cheese 1 tablespoon

- Cheese(Colby Jack) shredded 4 ounces

- Heavy cream 2 cups

Directions

1. Boil the pasta in enough water with one tablespoon of salt. Boil to al dente. Strain the pasta.

2. Add American cheese, heavy cream, Romano cheese and Parmesan cheese in a big pot. Over medium heat, melt the cheeses in heavy cream. Stir regularly. Do not let the cheese burn.

3. Broil the oven on high.

4. Transfer the cooked pasta into a baking dish of 9 x 13-inch. Pour the melted cheeses all over the pasta.

5. Generously sprinkle the pasta with the shredded Colby Jack cheese and put it under a broiler.

6. Broil the cheese until it begins to brown.

2. Best Spaghetti and Meatballs-Olive Garden Copycat

This famous recipe makes a big lot and is perfect for a big company. A recipe everyone will rave for!

Prep Time: 30 minutes | Cook Time: 2 hours

Calories: 519 kcal | Servings: 16

Ingredients

- Olive oil 2 tablespoons

- Onions, chopped 1 1/2 cups.

- Garlic, minced 3 cloves

- Tomato paste 2 cans (12 oz. Each)

- Water 3 cups

- Tomato sauce 1 can (29 oz.)

- Fresh parsley minced 1/3 cup

- Salt 2 teaspoons

- Dried basil 1 tablespoon

- Pepper 1/2 teaspoon

For meatballs:

- Eggs, beaten lightly 4 large

- Bread cubes, soft (chopped coarsely) 2 cups

- Parmesan cheese grated 1 cup.

- Whole milk 1-1/2 cups

- Salt 2 teaspoons

- Garlic, minced 3 cloves

- Pepper 1/2 teaspoon

- Ground beef 3 pounds

- Canola oil 2 tablespoons

- Spaghetti, cooked 2 pounds

Directions

- Heat olive oil in a heavy pot over medium heat. Include onions; fry until soft. Add garlic; cook for one minute more. Add tomato paste; cook, stirring for 3 to 5 minutes. Add the next six ingredients. Cook until it starts boiling. Decrease heat; cover and simmer for 50 minutes.

- Mix the first seven meatball ingredients thoroughly. Add the mixture to the beef; mix gently but thoroughly. Make into 1-1/2-inch balls.

- In a large frying pan, heat canola oil on medium flame. Add the meatballs; cook in batches until brown and no longer pink. Strain the oil. Add the meatballs to the sauce, and boil. Decrease heat; cover and simmer until flavors are merged, about 1 hour, mixing occasionally. Serve over hot cooked spaghetti.

Note:

For a healthier version, bake the meatballs on a rimmed baking sheet at 400° until golden brown for about 20 minutes

---

3. Fried Mac and Cheese - Cheesecake Factory's Copycat

This Cheesecake Factory's copycat Fried Mac and Cheese is very yummy! It's made from a rich mac and cheese in a tasty and crisp breading.

Prep Time: 10 minutes | Cook Time: 25 minutes

Calories: 387 kcal | Servings: 16

Ingredients

- Elbow macaroni 1 lb.

- Unsalted butter 2 tbsp.

- All-purpose flour 2 tbsp.

- Milk warmed, 2 cups + for egg wash2 tbsp.

- Cheddar grated 1 lb.

- Smoked Gouda grated 1 lb.

- Pepper to taste

- Salt to taste

- Eggs 3 large

- Seasoned bread crumbs 4 cups

- Alfredo or marinara sauce for dipping

- Vegetable oil for frying

Directions

1. Boil the macaroni as directed. Then strain and wash with cold water. Strain again and put aside.

2. In a saucepan, melt butter over medium heat. Add in flour and whisk, cooking for two minutes. Add in warm milk, keep whisking to work out any lumps. Cook until the sauce

has thickened for about two minutes. Take off from the heat. Stir in both the cheeses and stir until smooth and melted. Sprinkle salt and pepper to taste. Mix in the macaroni noodles, transfer to a shallow dish, and chill for about 2 hours until the macaroni is cold.

3. Form the chilled mac and cheese mixture into balls of about 1 ½ inch and put them on a tray lined with waxed paper. Keep in the freezer overnight.

4. In a deep bowl, beat together the eggs and two tablespoons of milk. In another bowl, pour the bread crumbs.

5. Take prepared balls out of the freezer. Dunk the frozen balls in the egg mixture, then roll in the bread crumbs, again dip into the egg and then again roll in breadcrumbs. Do these steps with each ball. It will give the balls a nice thick coat. Place in the freezer again until ready for serving.

6. Deep fry the mac and cheese balls until golden brown for 5 minutes, make sure the center is hot. Serve along with your fave Alfredo or marinara sauce for dipping.

4. Chow Mein – P.E. Copycat

This Copycat Chow Mein from Panda Express is simple to make and can be prepared in 20 minutes flat. And it is also economical!

Prep Time: 5 minutes | Cook Time: 15 minutes

Calories: 305 kcal | Servings: 6

Ingredients

- Chinese noodles, cooked as per package instructions 1 pkg. (14 oz.)
- Vegetable oil 3 tablespoons
- Celery cut diagonally
- 3 large stalks
- Oyster sauce 1 tablespoons
- Cabbage chopped thinly 2 cups

- Soy sauce 2 Tablespoons

- Yellow onion sliced ½

- Garlic minced 3 large cloves

Directions

1. Preheat a large deep skillet or pan, add oil. Heat the oil until it is shimmering, for about 30 to 45 seconds.

2. Add onion, cabbage, and celery and cook, stirring continuously, until the onions are translucent and the vegetables are a bit browned for about 4 minutes.

3. Put the garlic in and stir continuously for 30 to 60 seconds or until aromatic.

4. Stir in the cooked noodles. Add in the oyster sauce, soy sauce and cook, stirring and tossing continuously until the veggies and noodles are coated with the sauces and the noodles are thoroughly heated.

Serve immediately.

5. Pasta Fagioli - Olive Garden Copycat

Prep Time: 10 minutes | Cook Time: 5 minutes

Calories: 325 kcal | Servings: 8

Ingredients

- Ground beef 1 pound

- Yellow onion, diced 1

- Garlic, minced 4 cloves

- Carrots, peeled and diced 3

- Kidney beans drained 1 can (15 oz.)

- Celery stalks, diced 2

- White (cannellini) beans, drained 1 can (15 oz.)

- Chicken broth 3 cups

- Diced tomatoes 1 can (15 oz.)

- Oregano dried 1 tsp

- Tomato sauce 2 cans (15 oz.)

- Thyme leaves dried 1 tsp

- Ditalini pasta 1 cup

- Pepper, to taste

- Salt, to taste

- Parsley, finely chopped optional

- Parmesan, grated optional

Directions

1. Preheat a large stockpot or a Dutch oven over medium heat.

2. Put in the ground beef, minced garlic, onion, celery, carrots, sprinkle pepper and salt to taste, and cook until browned and no longer pink (for about 5 minutes). Strain the oiliness out.

3. Add to the beef mix the tomato sauce, kidney beans, diced tomatoes, white beans, chicken broth, thyme and oregano, leaves into the pot. Mix to combine.

4. As the liquid begins to boil, stir in the pasta.

5. Decrease heat and let it cook for about 10 minutes, or until the pasta is cooked.

6. Sprinkle grated parmesan and chopped parsley on top, if desired.

6. Mc Cheesy - Cracker Barrel Copycat

This copycat mac and cheese is served in Cracker Barrel with a biscuit on the side.

Prep Time: 10 minutes | Cook Time: 5 minutes

Calories: 425cal | Servings: 6

Ingredients

- Butter 1/3 cup

- Dry macaroni 2 cups

- Flour 1/3 cup

- Colby cheese, shredded 2 1/2 cups

- Milk 2 cups

- Salt 1 tsp

Directions

1. Cook the macaroni in a large pot of boiling water. Drain when cooked.

2. Prepare the broiler.

3. In a cast-iron skillet, heat butter on medium-low flame

4. When the butter melts fully, add in the flour. Mix together until both are fully combined.

5. Gradually pour in the milk and keep whisking. Add a small amount of milk at a time while continuously whisking. It will become very thick at first. When all the milk is slowly poured, it will form into a creamy white sauce.

6. Add in the Colby cheese, saving half a cup for the next step, keep mixing until the cheese is completely melted. Take off the heat.

7. Stir in the boiled macaroni. Transfer the macaroni and cheese into the cast-iron skillet, spreading evenly.

8. Scatter the remaining 1/2 cup of Colby cheese on the top.

9. Put the skillet in the broiler for about 5 minutes.

Chapter 7- Burgers & Pizza recipes

1. Healthy Mac and Cheese - The Best Big Mac Copycat Recipe

We're sorry, McDonald's, but this recipe is better, bigger, and a healthier version. We are huge lovers of the Big Mac and the general concept behind it. The small patties, the slice of American cheese, and the unique sauce are the popular components that enable this burger to symbolize the American fast-food chain. However, they cannot claim that the Big Mac is actually a nutritious meal. That is exactly where we fall in. The Big Mac's biggest problems are the low consistency of its ingredients and its middle bun's limited nature. We substitute the mysterious meat with healthy ground sirloin, which is then seared in a cast iron pan, browned and placed together in single, spongy sesame seeded bun.

Prep Time: 20 minutes | Cook Time: 15 minutes

Calories: 380 kcal | Servings: 4

Ingredients

- Olive-oil mayonnaise 2 Tbsp.

- Mustard 1 Tbsp.

- Ketchup 1 Tbsp.

- Grated onion 1 Tbsp.

- Sweet pickle relish 1 Tbsp.

- Worcestershire sauce 1 tsp

- Ground sirloin 1 lb.

- Black pepper and salt to taste

- American cheese 4 slices

- Dill pickle 8 slices

- Minced yellow onion 1/2 cup

- Sesame seed buns, toasted 4

- Shredded iceberg lettuce 1 cup

Directions

1. In a small mixing bowl, prepare the special sauce by combining the mayonnaise, ketchup, mustard, relish, grated onion, and Worcestershire.

2. Shape the beef into eight equal balls.

3. Flatten the balls with a spatula or your hands into thin patties on a tray.

4. Heat a big cast-iron pan on medium-high flame.

5. Sprinkle salt and black pepper on both sides of the patties.

6. When the pan is very hot, add the patties 4 at a time to the pan.

7. Fry for about a minute or a brown crust is formed.

8. Turnover, cover a slice of cheese on 2 of the patties and keep cooking for a minute and a half longer, till the bottoms have also formed a crust.

9. Place 2 pickles on top of each cheeseburger and also a spoonful of minced onion.

10. Cover the cheeseburgers with the bare burgers on top and shift to a plate.

11. Replicate with the other 4 patties.

12. Layer the bottoms of the buns liberally with the special sauce and apply shredded lettuce.

13. Assemble the burgers in the buns, serve.

2. Chicken Sandwiches - Chick-fil-A Copycat

Prep Time: 15 minutes | Cook Time: 6 hours

Calories: 430 kcal | Servings: 10

Ingredients

Marination

- Pickle juice ½ cup

- Sugar ½ tsp

- Black pepper ½ tsp

- Paprika ½ tsp

Sandwiches

- 2 chicken breasts, boneless and skinless

- Egg 1

- Milk ½ cup

- Water 2 tbsp.

- Flour 1 cup

- Powdered sugar 1 tbsp.

- Dry milk 1 tbsp.

- Baking soda ¼ tsp

- Ground mustard ¼ tsp.

- Pepper 1 tsp.

- Salt ½ tsp.

- Cajun seasoning ½ tsp.

- Peanut oil

- Pickle slices 8

- Buns 4

- Softened butter 3 tbsp.

Directions

1. Take a larger-sized Ziploc bag, put in all the marinade ingredients and the thawed chicken breasts in it and shake. Keep in the fridge to marinate chicken for about thirty minutes.

2. When the chicken has marinated, drain the marinade out. Slice each chicken breast in halves so you will have four thin slices. Place between two plastic wraps and pound till it is the thickness of about ¼-inch.

3. Heat enough peanut oil in a frying pan to deep fry chicken (about 1-inch). Beat egg, water, and milk in a bowl. Take another dish, mix the flour, dry milk, powdered sugar, ground mustard, baking soda, salt, pepper, and Cajun seasoning.

4. Immerse chicken in milk mixture, then roll into the next dish with the dry flour mixture and coat fully. Shake off the extra flour, and put it aside. Do the same with all remaining chicken breasts.

5. Place the chicken in hot peanut oil and cook until the coating turns a good, golden color, at least 4 minutes on both sides.

6. Heat a small pan. Apply butter on both sides of the buns, and put it on the pan to give it a light golden crisp color. Assemble chicken on buns, and add two pickles. Serve.

3. Crunch wrap Supreme- Taco Bell Copycat

Prep Time: 15 minutes | Cook Time: 15 minutes

Calories: 530 kcal | Servings: 6

Ingredients

- Ground beef, lean 1 pound

- Taco seasoning 2 tablespoons

- Queso cheese dip or nacho cheese 1 jar

- Mexican cheese blend, shredded 1 cup

- Yellow onion chopped 1 small

- Water 1/4 cup

- Corn tortillas 6

- Sour cream1 cup

- Garlic 1 clove

- Flour tortillas, burrito-size 6

- Shredded lettuce2 cups

- Tomato diced 1

- Cooking spray for oiling

Directions

1. Cook the onion and ground beef over medium-high heat in a large skillet, crumble the beef and cook until it's no longer pink. Remove the oiliness. Mix in the garlic, taco seasoning mix, and water. Keep cooking until it begins to boil. Decrease the heat to low and simmer for another 5 minutes.

2. In a microwave-safe dish, warm the queso cheese or nacho cheese sauce. On a large plate, assemble the flour tortillas and warm them in the microwave for 20 seconds.

3. Place one flour tortilla on a tray. Place half a cup of taco meat in the middle of the tortilla. Dollop 2 to 3 tablespoons of queso cheese on the meat. Cover meat with one crispy corn tortilla or tostada shell *. Layer a thin spread of sour cream on the corn tortilla shell. Top with tomato, shredded Mexican cheese and lettuce.

4. Fold the crunch wrap by starting with one end of the flour tortilla and bend the edge up onto the center. Keep folding the flour tortilla towards fillings in the center. If there's an open spot left in the middle, cut a piece from another flour tortilla and put it in the center to cover it fully.

5. Make all the tortillas in the same way. You will make 6 crunch wraps in total.

6. Oil a non-stick pan with cooking spray and heat on medium flame. Place each crunch wrap folded-side down onto the pan. Cook until golden brown or for 1 - 2 minutes. Cautiously, turn over and cook the other side as well until golden-brown. Do the same with all the crunch wraps. Serve hot.

Notes

When using corn tortillas, preheat oven to 400° F. put the corn tortillas on a baking tray and bake until crispy or for 10 minutes.

4. Burger Recipe - In-N-Out Copycat

Prep Time: 15 minutes | Cook Time: 30 minutes

Calories: 524kcal | Servings: 8

Ingredients

- Ground chuck, 60% lean 2 lbs.

- Vegetable oil 2 tbsp. + more for oiling griddle

- Onions chopped finely 2 large

- Pepper

- Salt

- Mayo 1/4 cup

- Ketchup 2 tbsp.

- White vinegar 1/2 tsp

- Sweet pickle relish 1 tbsp.

- Mustard 1 1/2 tsp

- Hamburger buns 4

- Iceberg lettuce, shredded 1 cup

- Tomato 4-8 slices

- American cheese or cheddar 8 slices

- Pickles optional

Directions

1. In a pan, add onions to hot oil.

2. Over medium heat, cook onions until they start to caramelize, turning golden brown, for about 30 minutes. Keep an eye on them to prevent them from burning.

3. Add half a cup of water and cook for another 5 more minutes till the water evaporates. Put aside, you can make these ahead of time and refrigerate.

4. Stir together the mayo, relish, vinegar and ketchup in a small bowl and put aside.

5. Shape meat into eight patties of 1/2 inch thickness and about 4 inches wide.

6. Heat skillet and spray lightly with vegetable oil.

7. Put the buns, split side down on the griddle and toast.

8. When the buns are golden brown and crunchy, spread the mayo mixture on the bottom bun.

9. Add lettuce and tomato on top.

10. Season both sides of the hamburger patties with salt and pepper and fry in the skillet for 3 to 5 minutes.

11. Spoon 1 1/2 tsps. mustard on top of the patty and turn it over.

12. Add cheese on top of the patty and cook until preferred doneness.

13. Put hamburger on the bun; add the caramelized onion on top. Serve.

5. Thin Crusty Pizza - Domino's Copycat

A thin, crispy pizza crust covered with pizza sauce and melted cheese. It is really quite easy. None of the bogus stuff! This version tastes as amazing as the original.

Prep Time: 10 minutes | Cook Time: 10 minutes

Calories: 340 kcal | Servings: 4

Ingredients:

For the pizza:

- Tomatoes, finely chopped (or Roma tomato 1/2) 2 Tablespoons

- Tomato paste 3 Tablespoons

- Italian seasoning 1/2 teaspoon

- Fresh mozzarella cheese, shredded 1/2 cup.

- Dried basil 1/4 teaspoon (optional)

- Balsamic glaze (optional)

- Pizza toppings of your choice

For the crust:

- Flour 1 1/4 cups

- Salt 1/2 tsp

- Water 1/2 cup

- Baking powder 1/2 tsp

- Olive oil 2 tsp

- Light corn syrup 1 tsp

Directions:

1. Put the pizza stone in an oven and heat up to 450 degrees F.

2. Prepare the crust:

3. Combine flour, olive oil, salt, corn syrup, baking powder, and water in a large mixing bowl until well combined. Shift to a parchment paper, form into a ball and spread it out thinly on the paper.

4. Prepare sauce:

5. Combine tomatoes and tomato paste in a small bowl,

6. Assemble the pizza:

7. Spread pizza sauce on the crust. Scatter cheese over it. Add your favorite toppings. Also, add basil and Italian seasoning.

8. Shift the pizza with the parchment paper to the pizza stone. Bake for 12 to 15 minutes, until crust is brown and cheese is golden. Let it cool for about 3 minutes, then slice and serve.

Chapter 8- Chicken Recipes

1. Chicken Piccata - Cheesecake Factory Copycat

Prep Time: 10 minutes| Cook Time: 1 hour

Calories: 422 kcal | Servings: 4

Ingredients

- Chicken breast 1 1/2 pounds

- Ground black pepper 1/2 teaspoon

- Butter 1 tablespoon

- Oil 1 tablespoon

- Salt 1/2 teaspoon

- Portobello mushrooms sliced 8 ounces

- Butter 2 teaspoons

- Salt 1/4 teaspoon

- Lemon juice 1 tablespoon

- Butter 1/4 cup

- Capers 1 tablespoon

- Dry white wine 1/4 cup

- Heavy cream 2 tablespoons

- Fresh parsley chopped 2 teaspoons

- Angel hair pasta (or any pasta) cooked for serving

Directions

1. Cut chicken breasts in half; it should be roughly 3/8 to 1/2 inch in thickness after cutting. Put the chicken breast in between two plastic wraps and pound it with a meat pounder. Carefully pound the chicken till it reaches a thickness of about 1/4 inch. Sprinkle salt and pepper on the chicken breast.

2. Heat a pan over medium heat, adding a tablespoon of vegetable oil and a tablespoon of butter. Fry, both sides of the chicken breast, till brown and remove from the pan.

3. Decrease the heat a little and add a tablespoon of butter, mushrooms, and a dash of salt. Fry the mushrooms till they just start to brown. Take out the mushrooms, add dry white wine to the same pan, and rub off the browned bits from the pan's bottom; it h a wooden spoon's help.

4. Include lemon juice and butter in the pan, and stir in capers and heavy cream also. Increase heat till the mix starts to bubble. Transfer the chicken and mushrooms back to the pan. Sprinkle fresh parsley and serve on top of cooked angel hair pasta or any other pasta of your liking.

2. Tequila Lime Chicken - Applebee's copycat

This version of the recipe is similar to the Fiesta Lime Chicken at Applebee's. It's a yummy Tex Mex meal idea that can be added to your weekly meal preparation for fast lunches!

Prep Time: 20 minutes | Cook Time: 20 minutes

Calories: 477 kcal | Servings: 4

Ingredients

- Chicken breast cutlets 4 (or chicken breasts sliced lengthwise in half 2)

- Olive oil 2 tbsp.

- Chili powder 2 tsp

- Tequila 2 tbsp.

- Cumin 1 tsp

- Lime juice 2 tbsp.

- Salt 1/2 tsp

- Garlic, minced 4 cloves

- Lime zest 1 tsp

- Tex mex cheese shredded 1/2 cup

- For Mexican rice

- Dry white rice 1 cup

- Chicken broth 2 cups

- Salt 1/2 tsp

- Chili powder 1 tbsp.

- Each measured 1tsp.

- Paprika

- Garlic powder

- Onion powder

- Cumin

- Butter

- Options for topping

- Tortilla strips

- Salsa or Pico de Gallo

- Lime wedges

- Sliced avocado

- Jalapeno slices

- Chopped cilantro

Directions

1. Heat oven up to 425 F

2. Combine all the ingredients for the chicken marinade together and marinate the chicken with it in a bowl or a Ziploc bag for at least 15 to 20 minutes. In the meantime, prepare rice by putting all ingredients for rice into a rice cooker.

3. Once the chicken is set to cook, assemble on a baking tray lined with parchment and bake for about 10 minutes. As the chicken is cooking, prepare toppings.

4. Take out chicken from the oven and sprinkle the grated cheese, again bake for another 10 minutes till cheese is all melted, and chicken is cooked fully.

5. Garnish chicken with toppings of your preference and serve with prepared Mexican rice. Enjoy!

3. Bang Bang Chicken-Cheesecake Factory Copycat

Remarkably crisp chicken nibbles drizzled with sweetened chili mayo – so delicious, you would like to double the easy recipe!

Prep Time: 20 minutes | Cook Time: 10 minutes

Calories: 532 kcal | Servings: 6

Ingredients:

1. Vegetable oil, 1/2 cup + more

2. Buttermilk 1 cup

3. All-purpose flour 3/4 cup

4. Egg 1 large

5. Cornstarch 1/2 cup

6. Hot sauce 1 tablespoon

7. Black pepper freshly ground to taste

8. Kosher salt to taste

9. Chicken breasts, boneless, skinless cut into 1-inch chunks 1 pound

10. Panko* 1 cup

For The Sauce

- Mayonnaise 1/4 cup

- Honey 1 tablespoon

- Frank's Hot Sauce 2 teaspoons

- Sweet chili sauce 2 tablespoons

Directions:

1. Prepare the sauce, blend together mayonnaise, honey, Frank's Hot Sauce and sweet chili sauce in a small dish; put aside.

2. In a large pan, heat vegetable oil on a medium-high flame

3. Mix together buttermilk, flour, egg, cornstarch, hot sauce, pepper and salt to taste in a large mixing bowl.

4. Taking one piece at a time, dunk the chicken into the buttermilk mixture, roll in Panko, and coat evenly.

5. Add breaded chicken to the pan in batches, and cook till crispy and evenly golden, for about 2 to 3 minutes. Shift to a plate lined with a paper towel.

6. Serve straight away, sprinkled with the sweet chili sauce. Enjoy!

Notes:

*Panko is a breadcrumb of Japanese-style and can be located in the Asian division of your resident grocery store.

4. Nuggets Recipe - Chick Fil A Copycat

This recipe helps you to get the finest, Chick-fil-A-style chicken nuggets you have ever tasted, with no need to leave home. These Chick-fil-A Copycat Nuggets taste almost as delicious as the real deal. Also, they can be prepared in only a few minutes!

Prep Time: 20 minutes | Cook Time: 5 minutes

Calories: 60 kcal | Servings: 20 nuggets

Ingredients

- Chicken breasts boneless skinless 2

- Milk 1/2 cup

- Eggs 1

- Flour 1 cup

- Powdered sugar 3 tbsp.

- Salt 2 tsp

- Pepper 1/2 tsp

- Vegetable oil

Directions

1. Start by chopping up the chicken breasts into small, bite-sized bits.

2. Pour oil into a medium frying pan and turn heat to medium.

3. In a bowl, add the egg and milk and whisk them until well combined. Put aside.

4. Mix the flour, pepper, salt, powdered sugar, and pour into a gallon ziplock bag.

5. Add in a few chicken pieces to the milk and egg mixture till well covered, and then transfer the pieces into the gallon bag and shake till each piece is coated evenly.

6. Fry the chicken pieces for 5-7 minutes on both sides or till golden brown.

7. Transfer nuggets onto a paper towel. Serve warm and enjoy!

5. Louisiana Chicken Pasta - Cheesecake Factory Copycat

Copycat Pasta Recipe as good as original!

Prep Time: 15 minutes | Cook Time: 25 minutes

Calories: 400 kcal | Servings: 4

Ingredients

Vegetables:

- Olive oil 1 tablespoon

- Diced red bell pepper 1/2

- Mushrooms 2 cups

- Diced green bell pepper 1/2

- Minced garlic 2 teaspoons

- Diced onions 1/2

Sauce:

- Heavy cream 1 cup

- Cajun seasoning 2 tablespoons

- Chicken stock 1/2 cup

- Lemon pepper 1 tablespoon

- Onion powder 1/2 teaspoon

- Chopped parsley 1 tablespoon

- Oregano 1/2 teaspoon

- Shredded parmesan 1/4 cup

- Salt (to taste)

- Fresh or dried basil (optional)

- Chicken pasta:

- Italian breadcrumbs 3/4 cups

- Chicken breasts (halved) 2 large

- Egg 1 large

- Parmesan, grated 1/4 cup

- Italian dressing 1 tablespoon

- Salt

- Red chili flakes (optional)

- Pepper

- Pasta of your preference

Directions

1. To a medium frying pan, add the olive oil on medium heat. Include the minced garlic fry for a minute, then add the onions, mushrooms, and bell peppers and cook until all are softened.

2. Now, add all sauce ingredients into the pan, including the chicken stock, heavy cream, Cajun seasoning, parsley, lemon pepper, onion powder, oregano, basil, parmesan and salt.

3. Boil the mixture till it gets thick, then take off from the heat.

4. Beat the egg, pepper and salt in a small bowl. Put aside.

5. In another bowl, mix together the parmesan, Italian breadcrumbs, and Italian dressing.

6. Boil the pasta in salted water.

7. As the pasta is being cooked, coat the chicken breast halves in the egg mixture, and then roll them in the breadcrumb mixture. Repeat till all the pieces are fully coated.

8. Deep fry the chicken breasts in oil till golden brown on all sides and cooked thoroughly.

9. Stir the boiled and drained pasta into the thickened cream sauce.

10. Cut the fried chicken into thick strips and lay them on top of your pasta.

11. Garnish with chili flakes and parmesan, and enjoy!

Chapter 9- Seafood Recipes

1. Fish Batter - Long John Silver's Copycat

This copycat Fish Batter recipe from Long John Silvers is spot-on for fish and so many other items

Prep Time: 15 minutes | Cook Time: 10 minutes

Calories: 458 kcal | Servings: 6

Ingredients

- Flour 2 cups

- Cod, cut into 3 oz. pieces (or any fish) 2 pounds

- Baking powder 1/2 teaspoon

- Sugar 2 teaspoons

- Baking soda 1/2 teaspoon

- Salt 2 teaspoons

- Onion salt 1/2 teaspoon

- Corn starch 1/4 cup

- Paprika 1/2 teaspoon

- Club soda 16 ounces

- Ground black pepper 1/4 teaspoon

- Oil for deep frying

Directions

1. In a heavy pot, heat vegetable oil for deep frying until the temperature touches 350 degrees F.

2. Prepare the batter by mixing flour, sugar, corn starch, baking powder, salt, onion salt, baking soda, ground black pepper and paprika. Stir all these ingredients to combine.

3. Pour the club soda into dry ingredients. It will start to foam; keep stirring.

4. Dunk fish pieces into the batter to coat well. Then drop the batter coated fish into the hot oil. For 2 to 4 minutes, fry the fish until the batter is crisp and golden; when done, the fish will float up. Strain fried fish on a wire shelf to drain excess oil.

Note:

You can substitute beer for the club soda to get a great flavor.

Got a little leftover batter? Cut up some onion into rings, and fry onion rings.

2. Shrimp Scampi – Red Lobster Copycat

This exquisite scampi recipe is simple to cook and is perfect for serving for an elegant company dinner. The tart lemon and peppery herbs complement the shrimp. Serve with the pasta and brace the compliments.

Prep Time: 15 minutes | Cook Time: 10 minutes

Calories: 395 kcal | Servings: 4

Ingredients

- Garlic, minced 3 to 4 cloves

- Butter, cubed 1/4 cup

- Shrimp, uncooked, medium-sized, peeled & deveined 1 pound

- Lemon juice 1/4 cup

- Pepper 1/2 teaspoon

- Olive oil 1/4 cup

- Dried oregano 1/4 teaspoon

- Parmesan cheese grated 1/2 cup

- Dry bread crumbs 1/4 cup

- Fresh parsley, minced 1/4 cup

- Angel hair pasta, cooked

Directions

1. Take an ovenproof skillet (10-in) to heat butter and sauté garlic until fragrant.

2. Include the shrimp, oregano, lemon juice, pepper; cook and stir until shrimp are nice and pink. Scatter with bread crumbs, cheese, and parsley.

3. Broil for 2 to 3 minutes keeping 6 in. away from the heat till topping is golden brown. Top onto pasta and serve.

Note:

Frozen shrimp can be used too.

---

3. Barbecue Shrimp Orleans - Ruth Chris Steak House Copycat

Bbq shrimp makes a delicious entree or even an appetizer.

Prep Time: 15 minutes | Cook Time: 10 minutes

Calories: 1184 kcal | Servings: 4

Ingredients

- Butter 1 pound

- Black pepper 2 teaspoons

- Cayenne pepper 1/4 teaspoon

- Paprika 1 1/2 teaspoons

- Salt 1 teaspoon

- Dried rosemary leaves, whole (first measure, then chop finely) 1/2 teaspoon

- Garlic chopped 1/4 cup

- Worcestershire sauce 2 teaspoons

- Tabasco sauce 1 teaspoon

- Water 1 1/2 teaspoons

- Olive oil 1 tablespoon + 1 teaspoon

- Shrimp (16 to 20 pcs.), washed, peeled & deveined 1 pound

- Green onions chopped 1/4 cup

- Dry white wine 1/2 cup

- Sourdough bread 4 slices

Directions

1. Prepare Barbecue Butter

2. Place butter at room temperature to soften. In a small mixing bowl, add butter, paprika, black pepper, garlic, cayenne pepper, rosemary, salt, Tabasco sauce, Worcestershire sauce, and water.

3. On a high-speed setting, beat the butter mixture for at least 3 minutes or till well blended. Chill to 40 degrees F approximately.

4. Prepare the Shrimp

5. The shrimp recipe will use 1 cup of the barbecue butter; reserve the extra for another use.

6. Heat frying pan on a medium-high flame, add olive oil. When heated, add the shrimp and fry one side for 1 to 2 minutes. (Do not overcrowd the pan. A large pan will hold about a pound of shrimps.)

7. Decrease the heat to medium, flipping the shrimps and adding the chopped green onions. Fry for an additional 1 to 2 minutes.

8. Include white wine in the shrimp pan and cook till it reduces to 1/4 cup. Mix in a cup of the chilled barbecue butter, turning down the heat to low. Cook, stirring regularly, till shrimp are about done (thoroughly white but moist and tender, for about 1 1/2 minutes). Watch out not to overdo the shrimp.

Serve right away in a warm dish.

4. Coconut Shrimp Parrot Bay -Red Lobster Copycat

Make this copycat Red Lobster shrimp recipe at home easily.

Prep Time: 15 minutes | Cook Time: 10 minutes

Calories: 416 kcal | Servings: 4

Ingredients

- Shrimp, large size (butterfly the shrimp) 1/2 pound

- Coconut flakes sweetened 1 cup

- Bread crumbs, plain 1 cup

- Cornstarch 1/2 cup + 1/4 cup

- Powdered sugar 1 tablespoon

- Mix of Pina colada 1/2 cup

- Spiced Rum 3 tablespoons

Directions

1. Combine the coconut, bread crumbs, and 1/4 cup of cornstarch in a large bowl, and put aside.

2. Mix together powdered sugar, Pina colada powder, and the rum in another small bowl and put aside. Keep half cup cornstarch separately in a bowl.

3. Heat the oil. The temperature should reach to 375 degrees F for deep frying the shrimp. Dip the shrimp in coatings twice as follows: for deep frying

4. First coat with cornstarch, then dip in the Pina colada blend, then roll in bread crumb and coconut mixture.

5. The second coating, again dip into the Pina colada blend and then coat with bread crumb and coconut mixture.

6. Fry the coated shrimp carefully in the hot oil until crisp and golden brown. Take out from the pan and drain.

Chapter 10- Beef & Pork Recipes

1. Three Meat Sauce - Olive Garden Copycat

This Three Meat Sauce recipe from Olive Garden combines pepperoni, Italian sausage and ground beef to make a tasty meat sauce absolute with any pasta dish.

Prep Time: 15 minutes | Cook Time: 30 minutes

Calories: 378 kcal | Servings: 10

Ingredients

- Marinara sauce (48 ounces) 2 jars

- Crushed tomatoes (16 ounces) 1 can

- Onions chopped 1 cup

- Olive oil 2 tablespoons

- Ground beef 1 pound

- Italian sausage, casings removed 1 pound

- Pepperoni finely chopped 1/2 cup

- Italian seasonings 1 teaspoon

Directions

1. Fry onions with 2 tablespoons of olive oil in a large stockpot. Once the onions become whitish and transparent, include the can of chopped tomatoes, two jars of marinara sauce, and decrease the heat to simmer.

2. Brown the Italian sausage and ground beef in a big skillet until fully cooked, strain the fat from cooked meat, and include the meat into the large stockpot with the prepared sauce. Add the chopped pepperoni into the sauce and beef mixture. Add the Italian seasonings into the mixture and let all of it simmer for at least 20 minutes. Then season to taste with pepper and salt.

Notes

- If you have a bigger family, try stretching the sauce with an extra batch of marinara or a can of tomatoes.

- Until all the assorted spicy minced meats have been added into the sauce, refrain from any changes.

- You might like to save this sauce and use it later when you have a smaller family.

2. Mongolian Beef - PF Chang's copycat recipe

A very easy and delicious copycat recipe to cook at home, and it also tastes ten times better!

Prep Time: 10 minutes | Cook Time: 20 minutes

Calories: 478 kcal | Servings: 4

Ingredients:

- Flank steak, sliced thinly across the grain 1 pound

- Cornstarch 1/4 cup

- Vegetable oil 1/2 cup

- Green onions, sliced thinly 2

- For the sauce

- Soy sauce, reduced-sodium 1/4 cup

- Brown sugar packed 1/2 cup

- Garlic, minced 3 cloves

- Fresh ginger, grated 2 teaspoons

- Vegetable oil 2 teaspoons

Directions:

1. In a medium bowl, whisk together 2 tsps. vegetable oil, soy sauce, garlic, brown sugar, ginger and half a water cup. In a medium saucepan, heat this mixture till slightly thickened, for about 5 to 10 minutes; put aside.

2. Combine the flank steak with cornstarch in a big bowl.

3. In a large saucepan, heat half a cup of vegetable oil. Add the beef and fry till brown and cooked thoroughly, for about 1-2 minutes. Shift to a plate lined with a paper towel; dispose of the excess oil.

4. Add the soy sauce mixture and beef to the saucepan on medium heat and cook sauce continuously to thicken for about 2 to 3 minutes. Mix in the green onions.

Serve hot.

3. Chili - Wendy's Copycat

Prep Time: 15 minutes | Cook Time: 30 minutes

Calories: 478 kcal | Servings: 8

Ingredients

- Garlic, minced 1 clove

- Olive oil 1 tablespoon

- Onion, diced 1 medium

- Celery, diced 2 stalks

- Diced green bell pepper, 1

- Ground beef 1 lb.

- Taco seasoning 1 tablespoon

- Pinto beans 1 can. (10 oz.)

- Kidney beans 1 can (10 oz.)

- Tomato sauce 1 can (10 oz.)

- Diced tomatoes 1 can (10 oz.)

- For topping

- Shredded cheddar cheese

- Sour cream

Directions

1. Heat a stockpot or a Dutch oven on medium flame. Include olive oil, onion, minced garlic, green bell pepper and celery. Once the vegetables begin to soften (in about 3 minutes), include the ground beef.

2. Break up the ground beef with a wooden spoon's help, and mix in with the veggies. Once the ground beef is cooked a bit and no longer pinkish, you can strain the oil.

3. Add in all the beans, diced tomatoes and tomato sauce into the stockpot. Add in the taco seasoning and mix it all together.

4. Leave the chili to simmer for about 30 minutes, occasionally mixing, so nothing burns or sticks to the bottom. The flavors will become much better if you let it sit longer.

5. Serve with sour cream and shredded cheese, if desired.

4. Barbacoa recipe - Chipotle copycat

Seared beef is slowly cooked in a delicious, fiery adobo sauce with a mixture of flavors that make the ideal juicy and delicate Mexican shredded beef.

Prep Time: 15 minutes | Cook Time: 6 hours

Calories: 378 kcal | Servings: 10

Ingredients

- Kosher salt, 2 teaspoons divided

- Chuck roast, trim fat 3-4 pound

- Olive oil extra virgin 2 tablespoons

- Bay leaves 2

Sauce

- Apple cider vinegar 1/4 cup

- Garlic 6 cloves

- Ground cumin 4 teaspoons

- Dried oregano 1 tablespoon

- Ground black pepper 1 teaspoons

- Ground clove 1 /8 teaspoon

- Chipotle peppers (canned, with adobo sauce) 4

- Adobo sauce (from can) 1 tablespoon

- Chicken broth (or water 1 cup + chicken powder 1 teaspoon) 1 cup

- Fresh lime juice 1/4 cup

Directions

1. Wash the uncooked roast with cold water and dry by patting it with paper towels. Ensure all noticeable fat is trimmed. It will allow it to sear and help keep the meat

from steaming so that you can get a wonderful flavor and a crisp coating on the external of the roast. Chop into 8 pieces.

2. Sprinkle 1 tsp of salt on all parts of the cut beef, saving the leftover 1 teaspoon. Put aside.

3. Combine all the sauce ingredients in a blender. Blend till smooth. Put aside.

4. Heat a heavy bottom pot on a medium-high flame until dripped water sizzles inside.

   Add the oil and sear all sides of the cut beef. Follow this step to guarantee adding coats of flavor. When the roast is seared nicely and has a good crust, take it out from the pot and shift to the slow cooker. Adjust the temperature of the slow cooker to high. Pour in the blended sauce in too. Add the bay leaves. Cook covered for 5 to 6 hours on high (or at least 8 hours on low).

5. About 5 hours later, shred the beef with the help of 2 forks to tug it apart. Stir to coat in sauce entirely. Sample, and add the leftover teaspoon of salt, if required. Cook covered for another hour.

6. To make burritos:

7. Assemble the burritos by layering Pico de Gallo, Barbacoa, and Cilantro Lime Rice on a large flour tortilla. Add toppings of cheddar cheese, Guacamole, and sour cream to make it even more exceptional.

Serve and enjoy!

5. Maggiano's Meatballs - Maggiano's Little Italy Copycat

This Maggiano's Meatballs recipe gives the perfect bistro-style meatballs in the cozy setting of your home.

Prep Time: 15 minutes | Cook Time: 20 minutes

Calories: 400 kcal | Servings: 6

Ingredients

- Ground beef 20 ounces

- Garlic minced 6-8 cloves

- Milk 8 tablespoons

- Egg 1

- Parsley, chopped finely 2 tablespoons

- Parmesan cheese freshly grated 1/2 cup

- Fresh basil chopped finely 2 tablespoons

- Seasoned bread crumbs 3/4 cups

- Salt 1 teaspoon

- Black pepper 1 teaspoon

- Olive oil 2 tablespoons

Directions

1. Heat oven up to 350F.

2. Combine bread crumbs with parmesan cheese, garlic, pepper and salt in a medium mixing bowl. When combined, include beef, milk, egg, parsley and basil. Combine well by hand till all the ingredients are very well blended. Alter the pepper and salt to taste.

3. Shape 16 equal-sized meatballs. In a large frying pan, heat olive oil on a medium-high flame. Fry the meatballs on all sides for a couple of minutes, until just browned.

4. Shift meatballs to a casserole dish and cook in the oven for about 10 to 12 minutes.

5. Serve with spaghetti and sauce of your choice.

6. Meatloaf with Ritz Crackers - Cracker Barrel Copycat

This copycat meatloaf recipe makes a flavorful, succulent loaf, exactly like the restaurant kind. Prepare this comfort food today!

Prep Time: 20 minutes | Cook Time: 50 minutes

Calories: 520 kcal | Servings: 8

Ingredients

- Meatloaf

- Ground beef, 80/20 (24 ounces) 1 1/2 lbs.

- Ritz crackers, crushed 1 cup

- Eggs, beaten 3 large

- Yellow onion, diced finely 1 small

- Ground oregano 1 teaspoon

- Green bell pepper, diced

- Finely 1/2

- Cheddar cheese, fresh shredded 3 cups

- Garlic powder 1 teaspoon

- Fresh parsley, chopped finely 2 tablespoons

- Ground thyme 1 teaspoon

- Whole milk 1/2 cup

- Worcestershire sauce 1 tablespoon

- Ground black pepper 1/8 teaspoon

- Salt 1/2 teaspoon

- Toppings

- Light brown sugar packed 1/2 cup

- Yellow mustard 1 teaspoon

- Ketchup 1/2 cup

- Apple cider vinegar 1 teaspoon

Directions

1. Heat oven up to 350 degrees F

2. In a large bowl, add ground beef, and with a spoon, break it into large bits.

3. Add all the ingredients in the "Meatloaf" list and mix well into the ground beef to combine fully. Use hands to mix everything perfectly.

4. Layer aluminum foil on a baking dish and foil with nonstick cooking spray. Shift the beef mixture into the middle of the baking dish, and make it into a loaf. The beef mixture can also be placed in a 9x5 in. meatloaf pan.

5. Put the meatloaf into the heated oven for almost 30 minutes.

6. Meanwhile, combine all the "Topping" ingredients in a small bowl.

7. Layer this topping on top of the meatloaf and keep baking for another 20 to 30 minutes. Bake till the top is crisp and golden brown and or till meatloaf is thoroughly cooked and checked with an internal temperature registers 160 degrees F at the center.

8. Take out from the oven and leave the meatloaf to rest for at least 10 minutes before slicing.

Notes

- The perfect meatloaf recipes use plenty of moisture from the mixture of lean meat and healthy fat. 80% is the optimal choice. Something leaner and the meatloaf would dry out.

- Using regular, cheese freshly shredded. The anti-caking agents in pre-shredded cheese make the meatloaf dry.

7. Pork Carnitas in Slow Cooker - Chipotle Copycat

This Pork Carnitas prepared in a slow cooker is a Chipotle Copycat recipe. A moist slow-boiled pork that's so tender and succulent; they liquefy on your tongue. Classic Mexican cuisine with simple and easy to follow recipe is impeccably seasoned that creates robust flavors.

Prep Time: 15 minutes | Cook Time: 6 hours

Calories: 507 kcal | Servings: 10

Ingredients

- Pork shoulder (also known as pork butt) 5-pound

- Kosher salt, 2 teaspoons divided

- Ground black pepper, 2 teaspoons divided

- Olive oil, extra light 2 tablespoons

- Ground thyme 1 /2 teaspoon

- Dried bay leaves 4

- Dried rosemary (or fresh rosemary sprigs 3 large) 1 tablespoon

- Water 1/2 cup

Directions

1. Wash pork roast with cold water. Using paper towels, pat dry (follow this step religiously, drying it will help produce less steam and make a better sear).

2. Heat a Dutch oven on medium-high flame. Pour two tablespoons of olive oil into it. Put pork on a dish and sprinkle a teaspoon of salt and a teaspoon of pepper on all sides. When the oil is glistening and hot, cautiously place pork in the Dutch oven (do not keep it for a long time, or the seasoning will start to draw out the juices). Sear all sides. Let the pork sizzle in the Dutch oven without disturbing it for about 2 minutes.

3. When it is properly seared, the pork will release effortlessly from the pan. If it sticks then, it is most probably not seared so far. It can take 2 to 5 minutes on each side. Decrease the heat if the pot gets too hot.

4. Place pork and bay leaves to the 6-quart slow cooker, carefully pouring in the leftover cooking liquid from the Dutch oven. Add another 1/2 cup water to the Dutch oven and resume the heat to medium-high. Scrape down the stuck browned bits from the Dutch oven's bottom with a wooden spoon or a silicone spatula. When the mixture starts boiling, add it to the pork. Add thyme, rosemary, and remaining pepper and salt into the slow cooker. Turn the pork over once to coat the other side with seasoning also.

5. Cook on high for about 5 to 6 hours with cover (or you can also cook on low heat for 10 to 12 hours). Once the pork is soft, shred meat using two forks. Try for seasoning; if needed, add salt to taste.

6. Mix the pork in cooking liquid to coat. Cook covered for another 30 to 60 minutes to have the pork absorb all the juices. Serve!

Notes

- Nonstick pans are not suitable for searing. Stainless steel or Cast irons are great substitutes to the Dutch oven.

- You can use boneless pork or bone-in, but look out for Cook Time:

- Searing the meat adds a layer of flavor. While you may skip this part, but it is highly recommended; the flavor and aroma are worth it!

Chapter 11- Vegetarian Recipes

---

1. Veggie Balls - Ikea Copycat

Rich, delicious, and flavorful vegetable balls that will taste like Ikea's meatballs. We added eight different vegetables, the same as in the original, with a tasty mix of spices and herbs to get the flavors just right.

Prep Time: 20 minutes | Cook Time: 25 minutes

Calories: 19 kcal | Servings: 50 balls

Ingredients

- Chickpeas 1 can (14 oz.)

- Frozen spinach 1 cup

- Carrots 3

- Bell Pepper ½

- Sweet corn (canned) ½ cup

- Green peas (frozen, fresh or canned) 1 cup

- Onion medium 1

- Garlic 3 cloves

- Oat flour 1 cup Olive oil 1 Tbsp.

- For Seasoning

- Cane sugar 1 tsp

- Salt 1 tsp

- Turmeric ½ tsp

- Ground black pepper ½ tsp

- Dried sage ½ tsp

- Dried parsley ½ tsp

- Nutritional yeast 1 Tbsp.

Directions

Prepare the veggies:

1. Peel and chop the onions, the carrots into quarters, the bell peppers into 2-3 parts. Peel the cloves of garlic.

2. Put all the chopped veggies into a food processor and process until they are chopped finely. Do not puree them completely.

3. When using frozen green peas, thaw them first and then cook them until soft.

4. Cook the chopped veggies:

5. Heat a little olive oil in a frying pan. Add the chopped veggies and cook for about 10 minutes. Cook until the veggies are soft and tender but not mushy.

6. Now include the spinach (if using frozen thaw first), dried parsley and dried sage. Stir and let cook for 1 to 2 minutes on high heat. Put aside to cool.

Prepare veggie ball mixture:

1. Add the drained can of chickpeas and the cooled pre-cooked veggies into a food processor. Process till both are combined. Do not puree the chickpeas; they should be in small chunks.

2. In a large mixing bowl, transfer the veggie mixture, sweet corns, cooked green peas, and seasoning ingredients. Combine well with a spoon or a spatula.

3. Add oat flour to reduce the moisture in the veggies. Begin with half a cup of oat flour and if needed, add more. The mixture should combine into a soft dough firm enough to make balls easily.

4. Using a measuring spoon, scoop up dough into a tablespoon like ice cream and form balls with your hands.

Frying

1. On medium heat, deep fry the balls for a few minutes till golden and crisp.

2. If using a true non-stick frypan, then the veggie balls will still get a crispy crust without any oil.

Baking

1. Heat oven up to 200 Celsius (390 degrees Fahrenheit). Put the balls on a baking sheet or parchment paper. Bake, for about 20 minutes until they are crispy and golden brown.

---

2. Jaipur Veggies -Trader Joes Copycat

Tender cauliflower, potatoes, green beans, carrots, peas, onion tomatoes, and a rich cashew sauce command this Jaipur Veggie recipe to be irresistible!

Prep Time: 20 minutes | Cook Time: 40 minutes

Calories: 610 kcal | Servings: 4

Ingredients

For the spice mix

- Raw cashews 1 cup

- Ginger, chopped roughly 1 inch

- Paprika 1 teaspoon

- Garlic peeled 3 cloves

- Cumin seeds 1/2 teaspoon

- Jalapeno seeded and stemmed 1 small

- Ground cardamom 1/4 teaspoon

- Ground coriander 1/2 teaspoon

- Ground cinnamon 1/4 teaspoon

For veggies

- Coconut oil 2 tablespoons

- Russet potato washed, peeled and diced finely 1

- Small cauliflower florets (all tough stems discarded) 1/2 head

- Fresh green beans diced 1 cup (around 10 -15)

- Yellow onion diced 1 cup (1 small)

- Frozen carrots and peas 1 cup

- Roma tomatoes, diced 2

- Ground turmeric 1 teaspoon

- Black pepper, fresh ground

- Kosher salt

- Tomato sauce 1 can (8oz.)

- Raisins 1/2 cup

- Coconut cream 1/4 cup

- Cilantro for garnish

- Naan bread and basmati rice for serving

Directions

2. Prepare spice mix: In a large frypan, toast the raw cashews for 3 to 4 minutes over medium heat, till lightly browned. Shift half the roasted cashews to the food processor. Coarsely chop the other half of toasted cashews and put aside for garnish.

3. To the food processor, add garlic, ginger, jalapeno, cumin seeds, paprika, coriander,

cinnamon and cardamom. Process into a rough paste; if necessary, add a couple of tablespoon of water to blend. Put aside.

4. Prepare veggies: In a large skillet, heat coconut oil over medium heat. Put in the cauliflower and potato; cook to softened and lightly browned for about 4 minutes. Add the onions and green beans; cook for an additional 3 to 4 minutes, till the onions are translucent. Put in the diced tomato, frozen carrots and peas, turmeric*, prepared cashew and spice mixture, and plentiful pinches of pepper and salt. Cook until fragrant for 2 to 3 minutes.

5. Pour the can of tomato sauce into the veggie pan, add a cup of water in the can and pour it into the pan again. Add the raisins and let the veggie mix come to a boil. Cover the pan, decrease the heat to low, and let it simmer for about 10 to 15 minutes, or till the raisins are plump and the potatoes are tender to touch.

6. Mix in the coconut cream, then let it simmer once again for an additional 3 to 5 minutes, or until the sauce has thickened to your desire. Add pepper and salt if needed after Tasting. Garnish with reserved cashews and cilantro. Serve hot, with naan bread basmati rice and.

Notes

*Turmeric tends to leave a yellow/orange stain; that's why it is recommended not to add it to any plastic bowl.

---

3. Marshmallow & Sweet Potato Casserole -Boston Market

Marshmallows & Sweet potato what a combination? Prepare this for the holiday feast and wow your friends!

Prep Time: 10 minutes | Cook Time: 55 minutes

Calories: 306 kcal | Servings: 12

Ingredients

For Sweet Potatoes

- Sweet potatoes washed & peeled(chopped into 1" pieces) 3 1/2 - 4 pounds

- Unsalted butter 4 tablespoons

- Light brown sugar packed 3/4 cup

- Ground nutmeg 1/4 teaspoon

- Heavy cream 1/2 cup

- Kosher salt 1 teaspoon

- Vanilla extract 1 tablespoon

- Ground cinnamon 1 teaspoon

For Topping

- Mini marshmallows 2 cups

- All-purpose flour 1/2 cup

- Unsalted butter 4 tablespoons

- Light brown sugar packed 6 tablespoons

- Rolled oats, old fashioned 1/4 cup

- Ground cinnamon 1/4 teaspoon

Directions

1. Boil the sweet potato pieces in a large pot of water over high heat. Cook till fork tender. Drain out all the water from the pot. Using a potato masher, mash the potatoes until almost smooth. Add the remaining ingredients (keeping the topping ingredients aside). Combine until well mixed.

2. Heat the oven to 350°F. Oil an 8x8 casserole dish (9x9 or 8" x10" works too).

3. Transfer the sweet potatoes to the casserole dish and even out the top. Sprinkle marshmallows on top of the sweet potatoes.

4. In a saucepan, melt butter on med-low heat. Add all the remaining ingredients of the toppings. Stir and Sprinkle on top of the casserole.

5. Put in the oven for 20 to 25 minutes till streusel (topping) is crisp and the marshmallows are goldish brown.

Serve and enjoy!

---

4. Koreatown tacos - veggie grill copycat

Prep Time: 20 minutes | Cook Time: 30 minutes

Calories: 325 kcal | Servings: 4 tacos

Ingredients

For the gochujang glaze

- Toasted sesame oil 1 Tbsp.

- Brown sugar 2/3 cup

- Garlic, finely minced 1 Tbsp.

- Rice vinegar 2/3 cup

- Ginger, finely minced 1 Tbsp.

- Water 4 Tbsp.

- Gochujang 1/2 cup

For tacos

- Vegan breaded chick'n tenders or nuggets (cooked according to pkg. Directions) 9–10 oz. Bag

- Black beans, slightly warmed 15 oz. Can

- Flour tortillas, slightly heated 4 large

- Green cabbage thinly sliced 2 cups

- Fresh arugula4–6 handfuls

- Ripe sliced avocado, 1

- Red onion, finely diced 2–4 tbsp.

- Creamy garlic vegan dressing

Directions

- Prepare gochujang glaze

- On medium-low flame, warm sesame oil in a medium-sized pot. Sauté ginger and garlic and soften for 5 to 6 minutes.

- Sprinkle the brown sugar in the same pot and stir until melted. Include the gochujang, vinegar and stir. Decrease the flame to low and let simmer for 20 minutes until reduced considerably. Keep stirring to avoid the bottom from scorching. Take off the heat and let it chill at room temperature. As the glaze cools, it will thicken slightly.

- Assembling the tacos

- When prepared to serve, toss a couple of ready vegan chick'n tenders or nuggets in the prepared glaze at a time to prevent them from getting soggy.

- In the middle of a heated flour tortilla, put a few spoonfuls of the warm black beans. Add cabbage; a few sauced dipped vegan chick'n nuggets; after that, add the avocado red onion and arugula.

- Dollop a few spoonfuls of the creamy vegan dressing. Immediately serve with some leftover black beans.

5. Lime Rice – Chipotle copycat

An easy recipe that is guaranteed to become a favorite in your house. This copycat Rice has a nutty flowery aroma and is perfectly smooth and moist. Having fresh cilantro scattered throughout and a vibrant citrus taste making it an excellent side dish that you can make over and over again!

Prep Time: 5 minutes | Cook Time: 25 minutes

Calories: 125 kcal | Servings: 12

Ingredients

- Water 2 cups

- Jasmine rice long-grain 1 cup

- Bay leaf 1

- Canola oil 1 tablespoon

- Kosher salt 1 teaspoon

- Cilantro finely chopped 1 tablespoon

- Orange juice 1 teaspoon

- Fresh lime juice 1 tablespoon

- Fresh lemon juice 2 teaspoon

Directions

1. Boil water in a medium-sized saucepan over high heat. Add rice, salt bay and leaf. Stir and return to a boil. When it is on a full rolling boil, decrease the heat to simmer and cook covered for 15 minutes. Take off of the heat, let stand for 5 minutes covered.

2. Discard bay leaf. Fluff up the rice using a fork, add the cilantro, juices and oil. Stir to mix.

Serve and enjoy!

6. Smoky Rosemary - White Beans-Zoe's Kitchen Copycat

An absolute side dish with a main dish or to be served as the main. It's very filling and hearty, yet oil-free and dairy-free that comes together in 30 minutes!

Prep Time: 10 minutes | Cook Time: 20 minutes

Calories: 228 kcal | Servings: 4-6

Ingredients

- Yellow or onion white, finely diced 1/2 packed cup

- Salt 1/4 teaspoon + 1/2 tsp extra

- Garlic cloves, minced

- Low-sodium veggie broth 1/2 cup + 3/4 cup more

- Homemade cashew milk 1/2 cup (see notes)

- Fresh rosemary roughly chopped 1 tablespoon

- Ground black pepper 1/4 teaspoon

- Liquid smoke 1 1/2 teaspoons

- Brown rice flour 2 tablespoons

- Cannellini beans, low-sodium, drained & rinsed 2 cans (15 oz. Each)

- Optional: drizzle of hot sauce for a spicy kick

Directions

1. In a small pot, add the onion with 1/2 a cup of vegetable broth and a 1/4 tsp of salt on medium heat. Take it to a boil, decrease the heat to medium. Let cook for about 8 minutes till the onions are soft.

2. Include the garlic and keep cooking for two more minutes.

3. Now add the extra 3/4 cup of broth, rosemary, plant milk, 1/2 teaspoon salt, rice flour, black pepper, and liquid smoke. Stir well to ensure the flour is evenly smooth.

4. Then, add the beans.

5. Increase heat to let to a simmer around the ends, then reduce to low and cover. Keep simmering for 10 minutes. Stir occasionally to keep them from sticking to the bottom. When creamy to your desire, serve immediately.

6. Optional: give it a spicy kick by drizzling hot sauce to taste.

7. Any leftovers would thicken up in the refrigerator overnight, so adding more broth will help loosen it if required and reheat on low.

Note:

- Prepare your own organic, homemade cashew milk, which is much creamier and more nutritious than store-bought cashew milk. In a vitamix, add 1 1/2 cups of filtered water and 1/2 cup of whole raw cashews. A process on high till absolutely creamy. That's it; there's no necessity to drain! Just use half a cup of cashew milk for this recipe. Enjoy all the extra with coffee, oatmeal, soups, and lattes for a creamier feel.

- A trick for cutting the fresh rosemary. If you have never clipped fresh rosemary, it's really easy. Don't cut the stem as it's too fibrous. With your fingertips, simply slip off the rosemary leaves, moving them in the opposite direction from the stem they grow out. They're going to slip straight off.

7. Veggie Fajita Burrito - Chipotle Copycat

Throw together yummy fast food in a flash with this cool recipe at home. Fajita veggies, beans, salsa, and rice, don't ignore the guac!

Prep Time: 10 minutes | Cook Time: 20 minutes

Calories: 597 kcal | Servings: 1

Ingredients

- Cooked rice, any kind, 3/4 cup

- Whole avocado 1/2

- Pinto beans 3/4 cup

- Lime 1

- Salsa 1/4 cup

- Cilantro, chopped 3 Tbsp.

- Red cabbage or romaine, chopped 1/4 cup

- Tortilla, extra-large 1

- Vegan cheese shredded 1/4 cup – optional

- Fajita Veggies

- Extra virgin olive oil, 2 tsp

- Red onion, sliced 1/4 cup

- Green bell pepper, sliced 1/2 cup

- Seasoning

- Salt, to taste

- Pepper, to taste

Directions

Rice:

First, prepare your rice. You may use several recipes. Cilantro Rice, Mexican Rice, lime and cilantro rice. Or go for plain rice, white or brown. Just make sure to season with pepper, salt and some other seasoning you'd want while using plain rice.

Beans:

For convenience, use pinto beans in cans! Rinse and drain.

For 2-3 minutes, microwave in a small bowl until hot. In the last thirty seconds of microwaving, add some vegan cheese. Or just heat on the stove.

Guac:

1. In a small bowl, add chopped avocado and roughly 2 Tbsp. of the juiced lime.

2. Add a dash of pepper and salt.

3. Mash. If needed, season with more salt.

4. Optional ingredients for the guac includes finely diced onion, minced garlic, garlic or even onion powder.

Veggies:

1. Heat a saucepan over high heat.

2. Add the vegetables and oil. Fry until soft and slightly browned, for 3-4 minutes.

3. Switch off the fire and season with a dash of pepper and salt. If needed, add more salt.

Tortilla:

Heat both sides of the tortilla over a gas flame for 10 to 20 seconds-do with care!

Another method: Microwave it to soften for around 10-15 seconds.

Assembly:

1. Add around 3/4 cup of beans, 3/4 cup of rice, romaine or cabbage fajita vegetables,

   mashed avocado, cilantro, salsa to taste.

2. For an extra vivid taste, squeeze a lime on top of it. Optional as well: Organic sour cream.

3. Roll the tortilla into the form of a burrito. Cut and serve on the side with extra salsa or spicy sauce.

8. Mixed Veggies - Panda Express Copycat

Mixed Veggies from Panda Express is a mix of zucchini, broccoli, carrots, cabbage and string beans steamed in chicken broth for added flavor.

Prep Time: 5 minutes | Cook Time: 5 minutes

Calories: 69 kcal | Servings: 6

Ingredients

- Chicken stock 2 cups

- Zucchini, cut into 1/2 inch semi-circles 1 medium

- Broccoli florets 1 cup

- String beans trimmed 1/2 pound

- Carrots, peeled and squared into 1-inch pieces 1 cup

- Cabbage, made into 2-inch squares 1/4 head

- Soy sauce or salt, optional

- Sesame seeds, optional

Directions

1. In a pot, heat the stock and assemble a steamer basket on the pot.

2. Add the veggies and boil the stock on medium to high heat.

3. Cook covered on low heat for 5 minutes.

4. Take out the basket; transfer the veggies to a serving plate. Serve.

5. Sprinkle salt or drizzle soy sauce for taste if you desire.

Chapter 12- Vegan Recipes

1. Vegan Fried Rice - P. E. Copycat

This Fried Rice becomes a great side or base dish for nearly all Asian dishes.

Prep Time: 15 minutes | Cook Time: 25 minutes

Calories: 78 kcal | Servings: 4

Ingredients

- Rice long-grain - uncooked 1 cup (or cooked rice 2 cups)

- Olive oil extra virgin 2 tablespoons

- Carrot chopped into small pieces ½ cup

- Fresh peas ½ cup (or frozen carrots and peas, 1 cup thawed)

- White onion diced ½ cup

- Tofu pressed 4 ounces

- Turmeric ½ teaspoon

- Garlic powder 1 teaspoon

- Tamari 2 tablespoon

- Sesame oil ½ teaspoon

- Ground pepper ⅛ teaspoon

- Salt ½ teaspoon

Directions

1. Boil water in a large pot. Pour the rice in and stir well.

2. Bring the water to a rolling boil and then decrease heat and cover.

3. Let it simmer for 20 minutes over medium to low heat. The rice will absorb, the water will become fluffy and light when it is cooked.

4. Transfer the rice to a flat baking sheet or into a large bowl to it cool off. This step creates more genuine fried rice.

5. Prepare veggies: while the rice is cooking, heat a skillet or a wok with a tablespoon of olive oil and heat to medium-high.

6. Put in the carrots and diced onions and fry for around 5 minutes. Take out and put aside.

7. Add one more tablespoon of oil into the wok and heat to medium-high.

8. Put in the tofu, garlic powder, turmeric, pepper and salt. Mix and cook for around 5 minutes, breaking the tofu into smaller pieces.

9. Include the sautéed veggies and cooked rice in the wok.

10. Stir and cook for around a minute. Add the sesame oil and tamari.

11. Fry/ sauté the rice and veggies mixture for about 5 minutes, turning and repeatedly stirring until mixture is combined well and thoroughly hot. While cooking, the rice will turn golden, picking up some of the tamari and turmeric.

Serve up.

2. Vegan Burgers with Vegan Spread - In-N-Out Copycat

Getting that authentic In-N-Out flavor with homemade vegan spread.

Prep Time: 10 minutes | Cook Time: 15 minutes

Calories: 228 kcal | Servings: 4

Ingredients

- Black bean or any vegan patties of choice

- Grilled yellow or white onion, 1

- Burger buns 4

- Tomato slices

- Fresh lettuce

For the vegan homemade spread:

- Raw organic cashews drained & rinsed 1/2 cup (soak for 2 - 4 hours)

- Almond milk ½ cup

- Fresh organic lemon juice 1-2 tablespoon

- Sea salt or pink salt 1/2 teaspoon

- Onion powder 1/2 teaspoon

- Garlic powder 1/4 teaspoon

- Organic ketchup 3-4 tablespoons (start with 3 tablespoons of ketchup, if needed, add more to taste.)

- Relish 1 tablespoon

Directions

1. Prepare Spread

2. In a blender, add the presoaked cashews with all six ingredients for the spread except the relish.

3. Blend till smooth.

4. Mix in the relish and chill for at least 30 min.

5. Check and add more ketchup or relish, if needed. To thin the sauce, add a little almond milk.

6. Prepare the burgers:

7. Cook the patties according to pack directions. To have an authentic patty taste, apply mustard on both sides and then fry.

8. Meanwhile, slice the tomato, wash the lettuce and grill the onions (instructions below)

9. Heat the oven to 400°. Toast buns by placing them on a baking sheet lined with parchment paper. Place in oven till browned to your preference or for about 5 min.

10. Prepare caramelized onion

11. Slice your onions.

12. Heat 1/4 teaspoon of refined coconut oil in a skillet or a pan, add the sliced onion.

13. Fry over medium-high flame until caramelized and browned, for about 10 to 15 min. Stir regularly and decrease the heat if required.

14. Assembling the burgers

15. Add the patty onto the toasted bun. Apply spread, tomato lettuce, and caramelized onions. Serve with slim-cut baked fries on one side, and, of course, extra spread.

3. Bbq tofu salad California-Pizza Kitchen Copycat

Try this CPK Salad- vegan style! The BBQ Tofu Chopped Salad with made at home Bbq-ranch dressing.

Prep Time: 20 minutes | Cook Time: 2 hours

Calories: 274 kcal | Servings: 4

Ingredients

- Lettuce chopped 8 cups

- Tomatoes, chopped 4 medium

- Avocados, chopped 2

- Black beans drained & rinsed 1 can

- Corn 1 cup

- Carrots shredded 2 cups

- Tofu drained & pressed 1 package (16 oz.)

- Bbq sauce divided 1 cup

- Mayo 1/2 cup (vegan if required)

- Soymilk 1/4 cup

- Chopped parsley 1/8 cup

- Powder 1 tsp. Garlic

- Salt & pepper

Directions

1. Cut tofu into small squares. Put in a bowl and add 1/2 cup of BBQ sauce to cover it. Mix to coat evenly. Keep aside for about 20 minutes.

2. Prepare the dressing: mix the soymilk, mayo, 3 tbsp. BBQ sauce chopped parsley, pinch salt & pepper and garlic powder.

3. Heat the oven up to 400 degrees F. place the tofu cubes on a baking sheet oiled lightly. Put in the oven for 15 minutes. Take out, turn over the cubes and brush the remaining BBQ sauce on them. Put back in the oven and bake for additional 10-15 minutes.

4. Assembling the salads: in a large salad bowl, place all the ingredients and mix them together. Or, for individual Servings: on each plate, place 2 cups of lettuce, 1/2 cup of shredded carrots, 1/2 avocado, 1/4 cup corn, 1/3 cup black beans, and one diced tomato. Top with 1/4 of the baked tofu. Serve after drizzling the salad with BBQ & ranch dressing.

Notes

Divide this recipe into four enormous salads for ravenous vegetable consumers or six normal-sized salads.

4. Oreo Vegan Cheesecake- Cheesecake Factory copycat

This vegan Oreo cheesecake is an indulgent dessert with a cookie crust and cookies throughout. Be prepared for awesome!

Prep Time: 20 minutes | Cook Time: 2 hours

Calories: 378 kcal | Servings: 16

Ingredients

For the CRUST

- Oreo cookie crumbs 1½ cup
- Coconut oil 4 tablespoons

For the filling

- Raw cashews ½ cup
- Coconut milk, full fat 13 ½ oz. can
- Vegan cream cheese 2 containers (8 oz. each)
- Silken tofu (see note) 1 container (14 oz.)
- Granulated sugar 1 cup
- Cornstarch 3 tablespoons
- Vegan butter ½ cup
- Vanilla 1 tablespoon
- Apple cider vinegar 1 tablespoon(see note)
- All-purpose flour ¼ cup
- Oreo cookies roughly chopped for the batter and topping 20

Directions

For the crust:

1. In a food processor, add the whole cookies and blitz until the cookies are coarse and crumbly flour. Put in the coconut oil and blitz to combine.

2. In an 8" springform pan, pour the cookie crumb and set to make a crust. Push it out evenly along the edges and the bottom of the pan. Put aside.

For the cheesecake filling:

- In a food processor, add the coconut milk and the raw cashews. You can use the same bowl that was used for the crust. Turn the food processor on and pulse for several seconds to crush the cashews. Take the lid off and scrape down any ingredients sticking to the side or top of the bowl. Again pulse up to a minute until the mixture is creamy and smooth.

- Add the tofu and the vegan cream cheese, blitz again till smooth.

- Now, add the corn starch, sugar, butter, vinegar, and vanilla. Blitz till you get a nice, smooth mixture.

- Pour the mixture into a large bowl, and fold in the flour. Then fold in half of the crushed Oreos and mix to combine. Put aside.

- Heat the oven to 325°f and let the filling rest for a couple of minutes.

- Once the oven is heated, transfer the cheesecake filling to the prepared crust pan and layer the remaining crushed Oreos on the top. Wrap foil on the bottom part of the springform pan to avoid leakage.

- Optional water bath: place the wrapped springform pan in a roasting pan and fill it with water up to ¼" of the pan .this process will prevent the top of the cheesecake from cracking.

- Put in the oven for 60 minutes, then turn the oven off and allow the cheesecake to cool in the oven for 1 hour. Take out from the oven, let it chill completely before placing it in the refrigerator, covered. Chill the cheesecake for around four hours (or even overnight) before cutting and serving.

Notes

- Use Earth Balance for vegan butter if available.

- Use raw cashews here without presoaking

- Silken tofu; packs are generally 12 to 14 ounces. This size serves just fine.

- Apple cider vinegar gives more depth to the flavor.

5. Ice-cream Cupcakes - Dairy Queen Copycat

Vegan-style Cupcakes prepared with chocolate, coconut, hot fudge, coconut whipped cream, ice-creams and Oreos! Can add non-vegan stuff for non-vegan people.

Prep Time: 5 minutes | Cook Time: 5 minutes

Calories: 536 kcal | Servings: 2

Ingredients

- Vegan chocolate ice cream divided 1 cup

- Oreos crushed divided 1/3 cup

- Vegan vanilla ice cream divided 1 cup

- Vegan hot fudge divided 1/3 cup

- Whipped cream (coconut) (for topping)

Directions

1. Take two small sundae bowls, place half of the chocolate ice cream in each. Drizzle a lot of vegan hot fudge, add handfuls of crushed Oreos, then cover with each sundae with a large scoop of vanilla ice cream.

2. Top these ice-cream cupcakes with whipped cream (coconut) and add sprinkles. Serving immediately.

Chapter 13- Drinks Recipes

1. Pumpkin Spice Latte Homemade -Starbucks copycat

Prep Time: 10 minutes | Cook Time: 5 minutes

Calories: 125 kcal | Servings: 2

Ingredients

For the pumpkin spice:

- Ground ginger 2 teaspoons

- Cinnamon powder 2 tablespoons

- Ground cloves 1 teaspoon

- Nutmeg powder 1 teaspoon (optional)

For the spiced pumpkin latte:

- Milk 2 cups

- Maple syrup 2 tablespoons

- Espresso 2 shots

- Vanilla extract 1/2 teaspoon

- Pumpkin puree 2 1/2 tablespoons

- Pumpkin spice 1 teaspoon

- Whipped cream for topping (optional)

Directions

1. Prepare the pumpkin spice mix:

2. Stir together cinnamon, cloves, nutmeg and ginger. Store the spice blend in an airtight container for up to 6 months. It can be used in recipes that need pumpkin pie spice.

3. Prepare the spiced pumpkin latte:

4. Heat milk in a small pot or saucepan (ideally to the temperature of 150°F-155°F)

5. Prepare and pour your espresso into a cup. Put in pumpkin puree and mix until thoroughly combined. Include the pumpkin spice, maple syrup, vanilla extract and mix again.

6. Froth your milk with a milk frother for around 30 seconds. Pour the milk on top of the espresso, heaping the fluffiest foam on top (use a spoon to keep it back while you pour).

7. Dust a little additional pumpkin spice and stir gently to blend, aiming not to disturb the foam.

8. Add whipped cream on top for an extra indulgence if you like.

2. Frosty Wendy's Copycat

This Frosty is just perfect in terms of consistency. Once you have successfully prepared this basic and tasty recipe, you would be flying on a chocolate-flavored cloud. With just three ingredients, this recipe is quick and fast to make.

Prep Time: 35 minutes | Cook Time: -

Calories: 425 kcal | Servings: 4

Ingredients

- Cool Whip 7 ounces

- Hershey's chocolate milk 1/2 gallon

- Condensed milk sweetened 7 ounces.

Directions

1. Pour in the Cool Whip and sweetened condensed milk in an ice cream freezer.

2. Then add all the chocolate milk, about. 1/2 a gallon and fill the freezer.

3. Stir all the ingredients with a long spoon and turn the machine on, and lastly, let it freeze for about 30 minutes.

4. If you desire chocolatier Frosty then top it with chocolate chips!

Note

For the closest match, use Hershey's chocolate-flavored milk!

3. Cherry Coke Copycat

Prep Time: 20 minutes | Cook Time: -

Calories: 128 kcal | Servings: 1

Ingredients

- Maraschino cherry juice 1 tablespoon

- Coca-Cola 3/4 cup

- Grenadine syrup 1 tablespoon

Directions

Mix together the cherry juice, cola, and grenadine. Transfer into a glass filled with ice. Top with cherries.

Serve immediately

4. Passion Lemonade Tea - Starbucks Copycat

Prep Time: 15 minutes | Cook Time: 5 minutes

Calories: 125 kcal | Servings: 2

Ingredients

- Lemonade

- Tea Bags, Tazo Passion 2

- Sugar 2 tsp

- Water 8 oz.

- Ice

Directions

1. Boil water on the stove or the microwave, or use an electric kettle. Pour out in a cup, add two bags of passion tea and steep for about 15 mins. Stir in two spoons of sugar or any sweetener you like. Leave it to chill.

2. To serve, pour two parts lemonade to one part tea over ice.

5. Pink Drink Homemade – Starbucks Copycat

Customize the sweetness to your desire. You will love the fresh taste of this drink!

Prep Time: 30 minutes | Cook Time: -

Calories: 125 kcal | Servings: 2

Ingredients

- Water boiling 1 cup

- Acai berry tea 4 teabags

- Coconut milk unsweetened 1-2 cups

- White grape juice1/2 cup

- Fresh strawberries sliced

- Agave nectar, optional

Directions

1. Add tea bags to a big glass jug. Pour 2 cups of hot water over the tea bags and let sit till cool. Take out the tea bags, squeeze and discard.

2. Add t white grape juice into the glass jug with the tea.

3. Add about 1 cup of the tea and juice mixture to a glass filled with ice. Add coconut milk to fill the remaining glass.

4. Garnish with sliced strawberries, and if desired, add in sweetener.

Note

All ingredients can be varied according to your liking. Want more coconut flavor to add coconut milk, decrease juice quantity if you don't want too much grape juice, and add any type of sweetener according to your taste.

6. Chai Tea Latte – Starbucks Copycat

Make this Starbucks copycat Chai Tea Latte in the coziness of your home and at a minimal cost.

Prep Time: 5 minutes | Cook Time: 10 minutes

Calories: 213 kcal | Servings: 4

Ingredients:

- Tea Bags 6 Black

- Water 3 Cups

- Honey 1/2 Cup

- Milk 3 Cups

- Cloves 1/2 teaspoon

- Cinnamon 1 teaspoon

- Nutmeg 1/2 teaspoon

- Cardamom 1 teaspoon

- Ground Ginger 1/2 teaspoon

Directions:

1. Heat milk and water in a saucepan on a moderate flame until it starts to simmer. Do not boil the milk as it can curdle.

2. Take off the saucepan from heat.

3. Add the tea bags, cinnamon, honey, cardamom, cloves, ground ginger and nutmeg.

4. Put the saucepan back over the heat and leave to simmer for about 5 minutes.

5. Take off the latte from heat and strain it. Serve immediately.

7. Caramel Frappuccino - Starbucks Copycat

Prep Time: 10 minutes | Cook Time: -

Calories: 175 kcal | Servings: 2

Ingredients

- Ice 1 cup

- Strong coffee, cold ½ cup

- Caramel syrup 2 tablespoon

- Milk ½ cup

- Caramel sauce 1 tablespoon

- Whipped cream

- Sugar (optional) 2 teaspoons

Directions

1. First, add ice, then coffee, ½ cup milk, caramel syrup, sugar, caramel sauce in a blender.

2. Blend until thoroughly mixed (about 30 sec.)

3. Pour into glasses, decorate with whipped cream and drizzle a little caramel sauce if you like.

8. Orange Julius Copycat

Prep Time: 5 minutes | Cook Time: -

Calories: 150 kcal | Servings: 4

Ingredients

- Orange juice concentrate (frozen) 2/3 cup

- Vanilla extract 1/2 teaspoon

- Powdered sugar 1/4 cup

- Milk 1 cup

- Ice cubes 1 1/2 cups

- Water 1 cup

Directions

Add all the ingredients into a blender. Blend on high speed till frothy and well blended.

Pour in tall glasses. Serve immediately.

9. Salted Cream Cold Brew Cold Foam copycat

Prep Time: 18 hours | Cook Time: 5 minutes

Calories: 175 kcal | Servings: 2

Ingredients

For Cold Brew

- Filtered Water, Cold 2 ½ Cups (20 Ounces)

- Coffee Grounds, Dark Roast, Very Coarse 1 Cup

For Salted Cream Cold Brew Cold Foam

- Cold Brew (Above Recipe) 2 ½ Cups

- Caramel Flavor 4 Pumps

- Cold Water ½ Cups

- Milk (Non or Low Fat) 1/4 Cup

- Ice 1 Cups

- Fine Sea Salt, 1/8 teaspoon

Directions

Prepare Cold Brew:

1. Add the cold filtered water and coarse coffee ground in a French Press.

2. Keep in the refrigerator to steep for 18 to 24 hours. Press and filter the grounds out.

3. Prepare the Salted Cream Cold Brew Cold Foam:

4. Mix 1/4 cup of cold water into 3/4 cup of cold brew. Add Ice

5. Add 4 pumps of Caramel Flavoring (preferably Torani) into each glass.

Prepare Cold Foam:

1. Stir in 1/8 teaspoon of fine sea salt into the 1/4 cup of non-fat or low-fat milk in a glass flask. Option: For extra creaminess, substitute half & half with half of the milk!

2. Froth using a milk frother until thickened

3. Carefully top the cold foam over the cold coffee

10. Shamrock Shake Copycat

Prep Time: 5 minutes | Cook Time: -

Calories: 390 kcal | Servings: 2

Ingredients

- Half-and-half 1/2 cup

- Vanilla ice cream 1 pint

- Mint extract 5 drops

- Green food coloring 4 drops

- Maraschino cherries (optional)

- Whipped cream (optional)

Directions

1. In a blender, combine half and half, ice cream, food coloring and mint extract and blend for about 30 seconds to 1 minute.

2. Add whipped cream on top & garnish with a maraschino cherry (optional).

11. Lemonade - Applebee's Copycat

If you assumed lemonade was actually lemons, sugar, and water, you could not fully get it. A shot of sparkling water is the secret to Applebee's truly excellent lemonade.

Prep Time: 8 minutes | Cook Time: -

Calories: 210 kcal | Servings: 4

Ingredients

- Sugar 1 cup

- Water 1 quart

- Fresh lemon juice 1 cup

- Sparkling water (e.g., Perrier, not tonic water)

Directions

1. Mix water, sugar and lemon juice all together.

2. Pour the lemon mixture into a tall glass. Fill up to 2/3 to 3/4, then add sparkling water until full.

Notes

An interesting alternative is to have some fruit (strawberries, raspberries, etc.) pureed with a little powdered or superfine sugar and add that to the glass prior to adding the lemonade.

Chapter 14- Dessert Recipes

1. Frosting - Cinnabon Copycat

Love the cinnamon rolls frosting at Cinnabon? Give this copycat recipe a try to get that delicious Cinnabon flavor.

Prep Time: 10 minutes | Cook Time: 5 minutes

Calories: 53 kcal | Servings: 6 cups

Ingredients

- Vanilla extract 2 teaspoons

- Margarine softened 2 cups

- Powdered sugar 4 cups

- Cream cheese softened 2 cups

- Lemon juice 2 teaspoons

Directions

1. In a mixing bowl, beat the cream cheese and margarine with an electric mixer on medium speed until well combined.

2. While beating, gradually add the powdered sugar. Once all the sugar is added, mix for 10 minutes on medium speed. Include the lemon juice and vanilla and beat until combined.

3. Frost cake, cupcakes or cinnamon rolls. Store any leftover frosting in a sealed container. It can be refrigerated for up to 2 weeks.

2. Chocolate Syrup - Hershey's copycat

You can practically replicate Hershey's chocolate syrup simply by heating some water. This recipe has a really basic ingredient list and takes about five minutes to cook that too at a fraction of the cost.

Prep Time: 10 minutes | Cook Time: 5 minutes

Calories: 125 kcal | Servings: 20

Ingredients

- Hershey's Baking Cocoa 1/2 cup

- Water 1 cup

- Pure Vanilla Extract 1 tsp.

- Sugar 1 cup

- Dash of salt (ONLY a dash!)

Directions

1. Over medium heat, combine the sugar, Hershey's cocoa, and salt in a medium saucepan, mixing well to combine, add the water immediately and continue whisking.

2. When it starts to boil, let it boil for 2 minutes precisely (no longer), stirring or whisking constantly. Keep a close eye on the mixture as it can quickly boil over!

3. Take off from heat, let it cool for about 3 minutes. Now, adding the vanilla, whisk well.

4. Keep the homemade Hershey syrup in a tightly capped container.

It can be stored well for up to 14 days in the fridge. The syrup does thicken significantly overnight once it has cooled absolutely in the fridge.

3. Lemon Loaf Cake –Starbuck's Copycat

This lemon cake Copycat recipe is crowned with a lovely creamy lemon and powdered sugar glaze.

Prep Time: 15 minutes | Cook Time: 45 minutes

Calories: 254 kcal | Servings: 20

Ingredients

For Lemon Loaf Cake

- yellow cake mix 1 box

- Lemon pudding instant mix (or 2 tsp lemon extract & instant vanilla pudding) 5 oz.

- freshly lemon juice 6 tablespoons(about 2-3 lemons)

- eggs 4 large

- vegetable oil ½ cup

- sour cream 8 ounces

- milk ½ cup

For Lemon Topping

- powdered sugar 2 cups

- butter room temperature ½ stick

- lemon extract 1 tsp

- Lemon juice 4 tbsp.

Directions

Prepare Lemon Loaf

1. Heat oven up to 350°F. Line foil on 2 loaf pans and butter and flour the pans or spray with nonstick spray. Put aside.

2. Mix all the wet ingredients together and beat until well combined.

3. In a bowl, put all the dry ingredients, add 1/3 quantity of the wet ingredients, and beat

   on low speed with a mixer for about 15 seconds. Now add all of the wet ingredients and beat for another 15-20 seconds on low speed. Try NOT to overbeat, or the cake will deflate.

4. Split batter equally between the two loaf pans.

5. Shift into the oven and bake for 45 to 55 minutes, until a toothpick put in the center of the cake is clean or until golden in color.

6. Take out from the oven and leave in the pan for 5 minutes to rest before transferring to a cooling rack and allowing to cool.

Prepare Icing

1. Beat together powdered sugar, butter, and lemon extract and lemon juice until supple and smooth.

2. Spread smoothly on top of both the cakes.

3. Let the glaze harden up prior to slicing.

4. Cheesecake - Cheesecake Factory Copycat

Prep Time: 10 minutes | Cook Time: 5 minutes

Calories: 298 kcal | Servings: 8

Ingredients

For the cheesecake

- Sour cream 8 oz.

- Sugar 1 cup

- Cream cheese, at room temperature 8 oz.

- Fresh berries, for topping

- Vanilla extract 1 tsp

- Eggs 3

- Cups water 1 1/2

For the crust

- Graham crackers 10

- Butter melted 5 tbsp.

Directions

1. Heat the oven up to 350 degrees F.

2. Put the graham crackers into a large zip lock bag and seal. Roll over the graham crackers with a rolling pin until they are crushed and flattened to a sand-like texture.

3. Add the melted butter to the crushed graham crackers in a bowl. Press them evenly into a spring form pan.

4. Put the crust in the oven for 10 minutes. Put it out to cool.

5. Meanwhile, beat together sugar and cream cheese with an electric mixer.

6. Once the sugar is put into the cream cheese, include vanilla extract and sour cream. Next, one at a time, add in the eggs.

7. Stop mixing once the eggs are mixed completely. Try not to overmix, or the cheesecake will crack while baking.

8. In a pot over the stove or an electric kettle, heat up the water.

9. While the water is heating, wrap aluminum foil on the bottom of the springform pan, then transfer it to a baking tray with edges.

10. Add the cheesecake mixture on top of the baked crust.

11. Cautiously add hot water to the baking tray, making a water bath around the springform.

12. Put the baking tray (with the cheesecake) carefully in the oven for 55 minutes.

13. If the cheesecake is slightly wobbly in the center, that's okay.

14. Slightly ajar the oven door and leave it there for about 1 hour to cool.

15. Then refrigerate the cheesecake overnight or for at least 3 to 4 hours,

16. Loosen the edges of the cheesecake from the sides of the pan with a knife or a spatula. And remove the springform pan's side.

17. Top with whipped cream, fresh berries, chocolate sauce and more!

---

5. Mounds Bar Copycat

Groovy, flaky coconut is wrapped in chocolate to make a copycat of the popular Mounds candy bar.

Prep Time: 5 minutes | Cook Time: 15 minutes

Calories: 170 kcal | Servings: 9

Ingredients

- Dark chocolate chips2/3 cup

- Coconut milk unsweetened 2 tablespoons

- Vanilla extract 1 teaspoon

- Coconut oil melted 1/4 cup

- Coconut flakes, shredded, unsweetened 1/2 cup

- Raw honey 1 tablespoon

Directions

1. In a double boiler, melt chocolate chips, adding coconut milk and vanilla, keep stirring.

2. Coat the mold with a pastry brush or spoon with melted chocolate. Chill for five minutes or till hardened.

3. Meanwhile, mix melted coconut oil, honey and coconut flakes together in a bowl to prepare the filling.

4. Take the mold out from the freezer and put a spoonful of the prepared coconut mixture into each hollow.

5. Top the coconut mixture with the leftover melted chocolate, put it back into the freezer to chill for five minutes, and enjoy!

6. Cola Cake - Cracker Barrel's copycat

This Cola Cake is the perfect dessert every chocolate lover dreams to create at home.

Prep Time: 20 minutes | Cook Time: 30 minutes

Calories: 234 kcal | Servings: 8

Ingredients

For Frosting

- Cocoa powder unsweetened 3 tablespoons

- Powdered sugar 4 cups

- Unsalted butter 1/2 cup

- Milk 6 tablespoons

- Vanilla extract 1 teaspoon

For Cake

- Flour, all-purpose 2 cups

- Dutch-processed cocoa 6 tablespoons

- Granulated sugar 1 ¾ cup

- Baking powder 1 1/2 teaspoons

- Vegetable oil 1/2 cup

- Coca cola 1 cup

- Salted butter 1/2 cup

- Vanilla extract 1 teaspoon

- Eggs 2 large

- Buttermilk 1/2 cup

Directions

1. Heat oven up to 350°F and oil and flour a pan of 9x13-inch.

2. Combine flour, sugar, cocoa, and baking powder in a big mixing bowl. Stir until no clumps are left and put aside.

3. Combine oil, Coca-Cola, and butter in a pot and heat till it boils.

4. Pour the cola mixture into the flour mixture and, on medium speed, beat for about 1 minute till combined.

5. Then add the eggs, buttermilk, and vanilla extract. Again beat until well combined, for about 1 minute.

6. Pour the batter into the oiled pan and place in the oven for 30 minutes .to check for doneness, insert a toothpick in the middle if it comes out clean or with a few crumbs, it is done.

7. Prepare the frosting as soon as you remove the cake from the oven.

8. In a pot, mix butter, milk and cocoa powder and heat it up till it starts to boil.

9. Take off from heat, adding the powdered sugar and then vanilla extract. Beat until smooth and spread over the warm cake quickly.

10. Cool the cake to room temperature. Slice and serve.

7. Dole Whip – Disney copycat

A delicious, creamy, sweet pineapple frozen dessert from Disney!

Prep Time: 10 minutes | Cook Time: -

Calories: 125 kcal | Servings: 4

Ingredients

- Pineapple frozen (ideally Dole brand) 2 cup

- Coconut milk 1/3 cup

- Granulated sugar 3 tablespoon

- Lemon juice 1 teaspoon

- Lime juice 1 teaspoon

- Salt 1 pinch

- Optional- sliced pineapple, for garnish

Directions

1. Add coconut milk, frozen pineapple, lemon juice, sugar, salt and lime juice in a food processor. Blend the ingredients till very smooth, and no chunks are visible for about 3 to 5 minutes.

2. Immediately serve the Dole whip in decorated glasses with dessert spoons or straws. To make the whip firmer, freeze for about 30 minutes and then serve.

8. Cranberry Bliss Bars – Starbucks copycat

These copycat Bliss Bars are totally delicious! One problem that I might see is that we have done a better job. A yummy Blondie cake with white chocolate, cranberries, and a unique orange taste, finished with delicious cream cheese frosting and drizzled with shiny white chocolate.

Prep Time: 10 minutes | Cook Time: 5 minutes

Calories: 325 kcal | Servings: 20 bars

Ingredients

- Unsalted butter softened 1/2 cup

- Light brown sugar, 3/4 cups packed

- Granulated sugar 1/4 cup

- Eggs 2 large

- Vanilla extract 1 tablespoon

- Kosher salt 1/2 teaspoon

- All-purpose flour 1 cup

- Baking powder 1/2 teaspoon

- Ground cinnamon 1/4 teaspoon

- Ground ginger 1/8 teaspoon

- Dried cranberries sweetened 1 bag (5 oz.)

- Chocolate chips, white 1 bag (12 oz.) Divided

- Soft cream cheese, 4 ounces

- Orange juice 2 tablespoons

- Powdered sugar 1 cup

Directions

1. Heat oven up to 350°F.

2. Take an 8 "x8" baking pan and line it with parchment paper and oil it.

3. Microwave butter in a big microwave-safe dish. When melted, add sugar and beat using an electric mixer. Next, add vanilla and eggs. Beat till well combined.

4. Add flour, ginger, baking powder, cinnamon and salt. Beat until just combined. Try not to over mix; otherwise, the bars will become tough. Fold in 3/4 cup white chocolate chips and 3/4 cup cranberries. Transfer batter into pan.

5. Put in the oven for 20 to 22 minutes till the center is set.

6. In the meantime, in a small melt leftover white chocolate in the microwave. Put aside. Mix powdered sugar, orange juice and cream cheese in a medium mixing bowl.

7. Beat until well combined. Add in half of the melted white chocolate, keep the remaining chocolate aside. Beat to combine well. Put aside.

8. Remove pan from oven and put on a cooling rack.

9. Apply the cream cheese frosting on the bars. Scatter the remaining cranberries and drizzle with the leftover melted white chocolate.

Slice and serve!

Conclusion

The social confinement induced by the COVID-19 has given rise to a great deal of culinary innovation worldwide. With so many restaurant dining areas closed, several food franchises and other companies have begun sharing recipes of their popular meals. They are all tasty and will help fulfill your quarantine appetite.

Many restaurant meals involve a range of harmful products. There is a lot more to it than what is in the food you ignore while consuming from a takeout container.

Check out these perks of preparing your dinner at home.

1. It allows a chance to interact.

Cooking together is a perfect excuse to hang out with your spouse or girlfriend. Another advantage of cooking is that, according to the American Psychological Association, practicing a new recipe together would be beneficial to your relationship.

2. It is proved to be healthier.

Many health tests have found that individuals who cook more regularly, rather than grab takeout, have healthy diets overall. These findings suggest that restaurants' meals appear to have more Calories: and fat than those eaten at home.

If you make items yourself or bring them together with services like Plated, you know precisely what goes into them. It will have a great effect on your physical well-being.

3. It is simpler to count the Calories:

The typical fast-food order varies from 1,100 to 1,200 Calories: in total – that makes up the entire daily recommended calorie intake of a woman (1,600 to 2,400 Calories) and about two-thirds of a man's calorie allowance (2,000 to 3,000 Calories). Restaurants have numerous additional Calories: per meal relative to some.

Making your own food ensures you can decide the food portions and caloric content. Recipes usually come with recommended dietary facts making it simple to eat the recommended quantity.

4. It is a time-saver.

It takes hours to get take out, and people have to travel to get it. Depending on where you reside, the time you order and how the delivery individual understands the instructions, it may take them longer to come so you can conveniently evaluate all paths.

5. It can even save money

In the long term, cooking food at home will save you money. A greater variety of products is supplied at a cheaper rate than in a single restaurant entree. It is better to get more Servings: out of a home-cooked meal than a takeout meal or leftovers for the next day. Savings can continue to grow rapidly after only a few weeks.

6. It is customized.

Eating at home offers you the chance to enjoy the things you love. Whether you like well-done meats or less spicy foods, you can make the modifications yourself.

7. It is fun.

When following a homemade meal schedule, you get to play with a range of recipes, sauces, and cuisines. You get several choices to make whatever you want. Preparing new foods for friends and family is a perfect opportunity to interact with them or enjoy a nice evening after working hard all day.

With practice, you can get great at cooking.

Manufactured by Amazon.ca
Bolton, ON

28831264R00079

'For Families all around the world. May the love within your family be so strong you will overcome any obstacles in your way.'

Family Life,

Family Love

Written and Illustrated by :

Tami J Quinn